Archaeological Sediments

A SURVEY OF ANALYTICAL METHODS

Archaeological Sediments

A SURVEY OF ANALYTICAL METHODS

MYRA L. SHACKLEY

Institute of Archaeology,
University of Oxford

A HALSTED PRESS BOOK

John Wiley & Sons
New York · Toronto

English edition first published in 1975 by
Butterworth & Co (Publishers) Ltd
88 Kingsway, London WC2B 6AB

Published in the U.S.A. and Canada by
Halsted Press, a Division of John Wiley & Sons Inc.,
New York

Library of Congress Cataloging in Publication Data

Shackley, Myra L.
   Archaeological sediments.

   "A Halsted Press book."
   Includes indexes.
   1.   Sediments (Geology) — Analysis.   2.   Soil science
in archaeology.   I.   Title.
CC76.S6S5   930'.1'028   75–1193
ISBN 0–470–77870–9

Printed in England

PREFACE

An archaeological sediment is a deposit which is directly or indirectly related to past human activity. This brief definition encompasses a wide range of sediments which have been directly produced, influenced or modified by man, as well as those whose cultural associations are more tenuous. Any sediment which has a bearing on the interpretation of a particular site, culture or human unit can thus be considered 'archaeological', even if it does not form an integral part of a stratified series of occupation deposits.

This book presents a summary of the analytical methods best suited to archaeological sediments, and is also intended to act as a guide to the techniques and technical literature of the subject. Archaeological sediment-ology is a very new discipline, since it is only during the last 20 years that the significance of the dirt surrounding the artifacts has been realised, largely as a result of the pioneering work of Dr I. W. Cornwall. When the pot, bone or other cultural debris has been removed on site, a vast body of evidence, in the form of a series of deposits, is left behind. In recent years other aspects of the palaeoenvironment of archaeological sites have received more attention, such as the molluscan, insect, mammalian and plant remains. The study of the sediments is still in its infancy, and it is hoped that this book will suggest a potential standardisation of approach and methodology.

There is at present little evidence in sedimentology of integration between excavators and 'specialists', contrary to the welcome trend towards co-operation with other branches of the environmental sciences. A study of the sediments is still regarded as a 'last resort' if the worker is faced with insoluble interpretative problems, and an unnecessary item of expenditure on an excavation budget. The role of the 'specialist' in branches of archaeological science is difficult to define, and two clear schools of thought seem to have emerged. The first holds the opinion that an archaeological scientist should be an archaeologist by training and a scientist by inclination, permitting of better interpretation of archaeological problems and direct feedback of experimental results into the main body of excavated data. The second camp believes in the application of scientific techniques to archaeological problems chiefly as an exercise in experimental versatility, which leads to the accumulation of a large body of information basically divorced from the interpretation of a site or archaeological problem. It is this latter approach which has been so strongly criticised by the opponents of the present trend towards the integration of archaeology with other scientific disciplines, since it involves a loss of the humanistic perspective.

It is hoped that the techniques described in this book will form a valid contribution to this branch of archaeological science, summarising available techniques and their applications. A 'cookbook' style has been adopted for the presentation of standard methods, in the hope that this will make them more intelligible to the non-specialist. The aim of the writer is to present ways of dealing with the problems provided by archaeological sediments, and an indication of the potential contribution of such studies to the interpretation of a culture or site.

1974   M.L.S.

ACKNOWLEDGMENTS

The following firms have kindly provided material for illustrations (together with assistance with many technical queries): Cambridge Scientific Instruments; Coulter Electronics; Engineering Laboratory Equipment; Evans Electroselenium Ltd; James Swift & Sons Ltd; Malies Scientific Instruments; Millipore Ltd; Pascalls Ltd; Pye-Unicam; Wild Heerbrugg.

I should like to express my thanks to the staff of the departments of Geology and Archaeology at the University of Southampton, both for the provision of laboratory facilities and for their resignation in the face of mountains of soil samples. I am indebted to the editorial staff of Butterworths for their help with manuscript growing pains; to Dr D. P. S. Peacock for criticism of various aspects of the text; and to Mr A. M. ApSimon, Dr D. A. Davidson, Mrs S. Johnson, Mr Philip Holdsworth and Professor B.W. Cunliffe for their assistance and encouragement.

CONTENTS

Chapter 1

INTRODUCTION

SEDIMENT FORMATION

A sediment is a collection of mineral or rock particles which have been weathered or eroded from their primary source and redeposited elsewhere. The following factors influence the nature and characterisation of a sediment:

(a) The nature of the parent material.
(b) The distance and means of transport.
(c) The depositional environment.
(d) Post-depositional changes or modifications.

All these agents are reflected in the composition of the resulting material, and can be detected in a controlled analysis. Archaeological sediments may be organic or inorganic, totally natural or entirely produced by human agency. They may have been modified *in situ* and can often be described as soils. However, standard laboratory methods of analysis are applicable to the wide range of sediments that may be met with. The available methods are culled from the literature of many different disciplines, especially geology (for understanding the nature of the parent material), geomorphology (for studying the processes governing weathering, erosion and transport), pedology (if the sediment in question can be considered to be a soil) and sedimentary petrology, which contributes many of the relevant experimental techniques. In addition, forays must be made into the literature of the biological sciences, and into certain aspects of mathematics and statistics for an understanding of the basis of sampling and the processing and interpretation of numerical results.

The development of a sediment may be expressed in terms of the 'steady state' concept of dynamic equilibrium. The system governing sediment formation is precariously balanced, and a change in one of the determinant factors causes the re-establishment of a new steady state. Yaalon (1971) concluded that many features of soil genesis could be explained in this way, by the need to reach and maintain a state of balance. The raw materials of a sediment are the product of an influx of material from different sources, including direct weathering products and material

1

contributed by biological, atmospheric and human agencies (*Figure 1.1*). These are then transported and modified by many different processes, including illuviation, mixing and chemical action, which may or may not include the removal of the sediment to a new site. If the processes take place *in situ*, then they are likely to culminate eventually in the formation of a soil. However, material is generally removed from the system by erosion,

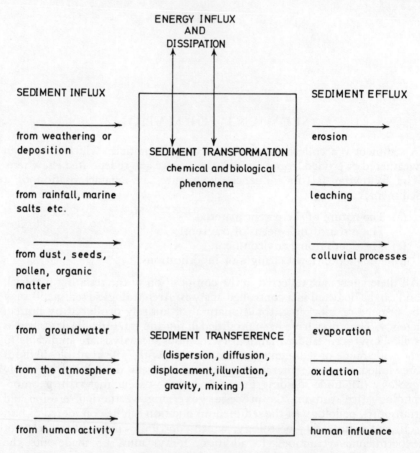

Fig. 1.1. *The sedimentation system (after Yaalon, 1971)*

leaching, evaporation or similar processes, and the sediment may often be redeposited many times. The particular state reached by the visible sediment system needs to be considered, since it will affect the interpretation of experimental results. A freshly weathered unmodified material will require a slightly different approach as compared with a sediment that has been subjected to a period of intensive weathering, or with one that has been much modified by man. The decision on a particular approach to further an understanding of the nature and structure of an archaeological deposit is governed to a certain extent by the nature of the sediment, but manifests itself more in the processing and interpretation of analytical results than in changes in laboratory procedures. The type of model shown in *Figure 1.1* is one where all the sediment formation and modification processes are active; however, it is equally possible that they may be dormant, as in a buried soil. The variation of sediments from place to place is directly related to the differential importance of these processes (Yaalon, 1971; Ruellan, 1971).

SOILS IN ARCHAEOLOGY

DEFINITIONS

Much confusion exists over the interchange of the terms 'soil' and 'sediment' in archaeological contexts. Numerous definitions of a 'soil' exist, varying from the simple ('a medium in which plants grow') to the more complex ('the products of the decomposition of the land surface under the influence of weather and vegetation') (Zeuner, 1959) and to the frankly obscure ('the result of the action of pedogenetic processes'). American geologists tend to regard the term as referring to all materials produced by weathering *in situ*, regardless of their depth or whether or not they have been penetrated by plants. For the engineer soils and sediments are lumped together as deposits which can be moved by earthmoving machinery without the need for blasting, and for the agriculturalist a 'soil' is only the weathered uppermost layers of surface deposits in which plants will grow. For the purpose of this book a 'soil' is taken to mean a deposit which has been weathered and altered *in situ* to such a point that a vertical section taken through it will show some interior zonation, a division into horizons which are the result of the movement through the profile of certain constituents. The soil profile zones are generally characterised as follows:

'A' horizon. Humus rich. Elluvial zone where leaching and other processes remove certain soil components by washing them through the profile.

'B' horizon. Illuvial zone where the materials removed from zone A become deposited.

'C' horizon. Chemically unaltered but weathered bedrock.

Subsidiary horizons are designated by numbers: thus, A_1, B_3. By these definitions all soils are technically sediments but not all sediments are technically soils. The more general term 'sediment' is therefore preferable for archaeological purposes, unless clear evidence of structure can be seen, since it has the advantage of not being ambiguous. Soil formation implies a period of stability, in which material is not removed by weathering or erosion and in which little new deposit is being added. Archaeological sediments are geologically very recent deposits, and may not yet have had time to form a profile (for example, colluvial material, loess, volcanic ash, cave deposits). Care must be taken to distinguish between a profile, which is an internal structure series within a uniform sediment, and a stratigraphic series, which may be a column of superimposed deposits of very different origin. The whole question of soils which occur in archaeological contexts has been admirably dealt with by Cornwall (1958) and Limbrey (1975). Soils are grouped together into classifications on the basis of shared characteristics, the classifications most commonly used being those of Kubiena (1935), the 'Zonal' concept of Baldwin, Kellogg and Thorpe (1938) and the United States 7th Approximation (Smith, 1960). Some recent papers on the application of soil studies to archaeological problems include those of Romans (1962), who studied the soil development at a Roman marching camp in Scotland; Shipley and Romans (1961), who worked on soils from a circular enclosure in Perth; Biek (1960) describing a Bronze Age buried soil from a Cornish site; and Arrhenious (1963), who analysed soils from old Indian sites in the United States.

PALAEOSOLS

The majority of soils occurring in archaeological contexts are palaeosols, namely soils formed in a landscape of the past (Yaalon, 1971). The interpretation of palaeosols rests on an understanding of how the soil-forming processes operate in modern soils, and at what speed (Burnham, 1973). In some circumstances processes such as the evolution of soil organic matter, the reduction of ferric oxide or the leaching of soluble salts can be very rapid. The leaching of carbonates from a thick layer or the development of a podsol can take several hundred years, but the formation of textural B horizons and of some thick chemically weathered layers may require 10 000 years (Bullock, 1973). Palaeosols include several different types of soil:

(a) *Buried soils.* Soil profiles or parts of profiles which are buried beneath non-pedological layers (e.g. volcanic ash, lava, loess, alluvium).

(b) *Relict soils.* Soils which possess certain characteristics which belong to a previous soil-forming cycle, different from the present one. Relict soils can thus be rather young, and many occur in Britain in late glacial Devensian contexts, formed in an environment quite different from the current one (Avery, 1974).

(c) The term '*fossil*' *soil* is rather ambiguous, and is applied to both buried and relict soils. Gibbs (1971) considers that it may only strictly describe soils which are not related to the organic cycle functioning at present, e.g. those which occur well below the current rooting zones of plants.

An interesting example of a Bronze Age buried soil has recently been described by Money (1973), stratified beneath pumice and ash deposits at Acrotiri, on the island of Santorini (Thera) in the Aegean. Money sampled a humus-like layer which occurred between the ruins of the Late Minoan

Ia town and the pumice and ash deposits produced in the cataclysmic eruption of the volcano on Thera which overwhelmed the island and caused temporary desolation in eastern Crete in Late Minoan Ib. The soil development in the area suggested a distinct interval between the destruction of the Late Minoan Ia buildings by an earthquake, and their burial by the later explosion. Analysis was carried out by Dr I. W. Cornwall, and showed that the accumulation of a thin layer of humus over the ruins was accompanied by the growth of some vegetation, later burnt *in situ*. The layer was capped after a substantial interval by a deposit of 'fine pellety pumice' ejected by a slight explosion of the volcano, followed by the pumice and ash of the main explosion. This occurrence is most significant since it had previously been difficult to explain the lack of Late Minoan Ib artifacts at Acrotiri, although these occur on the Cretan sites. Page (1970) suggested that the main pumice fall of Santorini was several decades earlier than that which occurred on Crete, a conclusion that was not supported by vulcanological opinion. The growth of the soil over the ruins of the Late Minoan Ia Acrotiri settlement represented the passing of these few decades, and resolved the chronological problem by explaining the lack of Late Minoan Ib artifacts at Acrotiri and removing any reason why the Santorini settlements and the sites of eastern Crete should not have been overwhelmed at the same time.

Bullock (1973) discusses techniques especially suited to the study of palaeosols, and emphasises the importance of particle size analysis in detecting lithological discontinuities and of detailed studies of the mineralogy of the fine sands and silts. Micromorphological techniques (p. 85) are suitable for the study of soil-forming processes in palaeosols, and chemical methods, such as amino acid analysis (Gohn, 1972), may be used to reconstruct the soil-forming environment. Federoff (1971) discusses the interpretation of thin sections of palaeosols, and considers that it is possible to distinguish between colluvial and undisturbed material. Thin sections also show features such as cryoturbation or contamination and the presence of diagenetic concretions (e.g. carbonates or iron oxides) formed after the burial of the soil.

Radiocarbon dating methods have been applied to palaeosols, notably by Ruhe, Miller and Vreeken (1971) and Gerasimov (1971), but this has to be done with caution since percolating groundwater may add a contaminant in the form of fossil or modern carbon, and there is always a danger that the sample may have been penetrated by recent rootlets or affected by carbonate deposits.

THE EXCAVATION OF SEDIMENTS

The first concern of the archaeologist is always, quite rightly, the recovery of archaeological information such as artifacts or other cultural remains. The recovery of actual human bones is an integral part of this work, but the total recovery of mammalian bones was by no means standard practice until quite recently. Even now there are excavators who refuse to keep all bone fragments, just as there are still some diehards who insist that only the base and rim sherds of pottery are likely to be significant. With the advent of increasing awareness of the significance of the site palaeoenvironment, a gradual process occupying the last 15 years, and the development of on-site recovery techniques such as sieving or flotation, the recovery of environmental evidence (grain, seeds, mollusca, small bones) has been much improved. It is rare, however, to find that any effort is made to systematically recover information about the sediments, although 'soil' samples are often taken at random out of a vague sense of duty. Unless such samples come from a critical deposit they are likely to be forgotten, since an analyst automatically gives such casual material very low priority. It is still common to find sediment reports tacked on to the end of excavation reports as appendices, little effort having been made to integrate their contents with the main body of the work. However, at the present date there is a move away from this system, exemplified by the works of Saucier (1966), Sokoloff and Lorenzo (1953) and Proudfoot (1963).

Figure 1.2 illustrates diagrammatically the processes involved in the

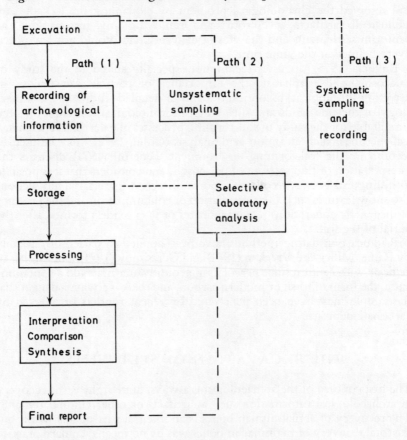

Fig. 1.2. The recovery of archaeological information

recovery of archaeological information. The information obtained by excavation is recorded in the field, generally in site notebooks, plans, drawings and photographs. The finds are then stored with this information for an unspecified time until a report can be published. During this time, which is not infrequently as long as 10 or 20 years, the data are largely inaccessible except by personal application to the director, who is perfectly at liberty to withhold them. It is only fair to say, however, that this latter eventuality seldom comes to pass nowadays, with increasing pressure from financial sources contributing towards the publication of speedy interim reports. However, the final stage of the process (Path 1), namely the interpretation of the site and a consideration of cultural relationships, may not follow for some years. The second possible data recovery method allows for a little environmental awareness, although only for the taking of unspecified samples. This results in the inclusion of a series of specialist appendices and little attempt to integrate them with the archaeology. The sampling methods employed are generally poor, and the whole system implies a lack of professionalism and of appreciation of potential technical contributions. The third possibility (Path 3) represents a step on the way to the sedimentologist's Utopia. Here the recovery of all aspects of site palaeo-environment progresses hand-in-hand with the excavation, ideally by employing a full-time team of specialists. This is, of course, extremely expensive, but a compromise can be reached by consulting specialist advice *before* the excavation to correlate sampling procedures and descriptions and to ensure that the whole excavation functions as a harmonious unit. The site sediment descriptions are likely to be accurate and meaningful, and the indiscriminate sampling plans can be avoided. There is no reason why such a reasonable set-up should increase excavation cost by an exorbitant amount, and it would certainly pay dividends in information feed-back and interdisciplinary co-operation. Ideally, the environmental data should be stored with the archaeological information for the final report, which is then able to present a complete synthesis. This method is not so unrealistic as it sounds and it would be fair to say that many of the better (more enlightened) excavators are already beginning to think along these lines.

The recovery of information about archaeological sediments can therefore be divided into four basic stages:

Stage 1. Field description and recording. This is carried out (obviously) on site, preferably recording information on standard forms, and assisting in the interpretation of 'problem' deposits and depositional sequences. The process is accompanied by information storage in the form of notes, drawings and photographs, and by selective sampling when required.

Stage 2. Sample pre-treatment. If taking a sample is deemed necessary and a laboratory analysis indicated, then this should be because of a specific query that cannot be answered in the field. When the sample reaches the laboratory it will require pre-treatment before the analysis can begin, generally consisting of splitting, drying and the removal of contaminants such as organic matter or mineral salts.

Stage 3. Analysis. The sample is processed by a standard series of tests and routine methods, aimed at solving the particular problem which is presented. The results of these processes are then combined with the information obtained in Stage 1 to give a complete interpretation.

Stage 4. Feedback. All sedimentological results are then combined with the data obtained from studies carried out on other aspects of the site palaeoenvironment, and the whole fed back into the archaeological data-processing system.

This book is obviously principally concerned with establishing a methodology for Stages 2 and 3, but some time will be spent on considering field treatment and sampling methods, which provide the basis for all later analytical work.

References

ARRHENIOUS, O. (1963). 'Investigation of soil from old Indian sites', *Ethnos*, **2–4**, 122–136

AVERY, B. W. (1974). *Soil Survey Laboratory Methods* (Soil Survey Technical Monograph No. 6, Soil Survey of England and Wales)

BALDWIN, M., KELLOGG, C. E. and THORPE, J. (1938). 'Soil classification', in *Soils and Men*, US Dept. Agriculture Yearbook, 979–1001

BURNHAM, C. P. (1973). 'Soil formation past and present', *Quaternary Newsletter*, **9**, 1

BIEK, L. (1960). Appendix I: 'The soils', in 'Craig-a-merrin: a Bronze Age barrow at Liskey, Cornwall', *Proceedings of the Prehistoric Society*, **26**, 76–98

BULLOCK, P. (1973). 'Techniques applicable to the study of palaeosols', *Quaternary Newsletter*, **9**, 1–2

CORNWALL, I. W. (1958). *Soils for the Archaeologist* (Phoenix, London)

FEDEROFF, N. (1971). 'The usefulness of micromorphology in palaeopedology', in *Palaeopedology*, cd. Yaalon, D. H. (International Society of Soil Science and Israel University Press, Jerusalem)

GERASIMOV, I. P. (1971). 'Nature and originality of palaeosols', in *Palaeopedology*, ed. Yaalon, D. H. (International Society of Soil Science and Israel University Press, Jerusalem)

GIBBS, H. S. (1971). 'Nature of palaeosols in New Zealand and their classification', in *Palaeopedology*, ed. Yaalon, D. H. (International Society of Soil Science and Israel University Press, Jerusalem)

GOHN, K. M. (1972). 'Amino acid levels as indicators of palaeosols in New Zealand soil profiles', *Geoderma*, **7**, 33–47

KUBIENA, W. L. (1935). *The Soils of Europe* (Murby, London)

LIMBREY, S. (1975). *Soil Science in Archaeology* (Seminar Press, London)

MONEY, J. (1973). 'The destruction of Acrotiri', *Antiquity*, **47** (185), 50–53

PAGE, D. (1970). 'The Santorini volcano and the destruction of Minoan Crete', *Society for the Promotion of Hellenic Studies*, Supplementary Paper 12

PROUDFOOT, V. B. (1963). 'Soil report on the henge monument at Nunwich', *Yorkshire Archaeological Journal*, **41** (1), 103–107

ROMANS, J. C. C. (1962). 'The origin of the B₃ horizon of the podsolic soils in north eastern Scotland', *Journal of Soil Science*, **13**, 141–147

RUELLAN, A. (1971). 'The history of soils: some problems of definitions and interpretation', in *Palaeopedology*, ed. Yaalon, D. H. (International Society of Soil Science and Israel University Press, Jerusalem)

RUHE, R. V., MILLER, G. A. and VREEKEN, W. T. (1971). 'Palaeosols, loess sedimentation and soil stratigraphy', in *Palaeopedology*, ed. Yaalon, D. H. (International Society of Soil Science and Israel University Press, Jerusalem)

SAUCIER, R. T. (1966). 'Soil survey reports and archaeological investigations', *American Antiquity*, **31**, 419–422

SHIPLEY, B. M. and ROMANS, J. C. (1961). 'The soils of the Dalnaglar circular enclosure, Glenshee, Perth,' *Proceedings of the Society of Antiquaries of Scotland*, **34**, 146–153

SMITH, G. D. (ed.) (1960). *Soil Classification—A Comprehensive System, 7th Approximation* (Soil Survey Staff, Soil Conservation Service, US Dept. Agriculture)

SOKOLOFF, V. P. and LORENZO, J. L. (1953). 'Modern and ancient soils at some archaeological sites in the Valley of Mexico', *American Antiquity*, **19**, 50–55

YAALON, D. H. (ed.) (1971). *Palaeopedology: Origin, Nature and Dating of Palaeosols* (International Society of Soil Science and Israel University Press, Jerusalem)

ZEUNER, F. E. (1959). *The Pleistocene Period* (Hutchinson, London)

Chapter 2

FIELD DESCRIPTION AND RECORDING

SITE RECORDING

A specialist cannot work isolated from the site. He needs to see the problems appearing and to advise and comment on recording and field-work. Excavation is often a fairly speedy process, especially with the current concentration of financial resources on short-term 'rescue' work, which necessitates close liaison between the excavation director and his environmental specialists. A surprising amount of information can be recovered from careful field descriptions, which saves a great deal of wasted laboratory time and speeds up the appearance of excavation reports. Ideally, the environmental specialists should be present for the entire duration of the excavation, but if this is not possible then much preliminary work is involved to ensure that the expected questions and problems are provided for and that there is a methodology for dealing with the unexpected ones. Adequate routine sediment description need not be time-consuming but will pay dividends in site interpretation. In many cases standard record sheets can be designed before the excavation, to cope with routine recording, and specialists need only be called to the site to deal with particular problems. Since the question of sample-taking is more delicate than is often supposed, most specialists will prefer to take their own.

It is neither possible nor desirable to record all aspects of the sediment-ology of a site, but a collection of selected characteristics can profitably be recorded. This standard procedure has then to be supplemented by laboratory analysis for particular points, bearing in mind that all detailed analytical work is time-consuming and expensive, if significant and repeatable results are to be obtained. Work on sediments does not just consist of the detailed analysis of a few samples from promising layers. Best results are obtained from a combination of adequate field recording and selective laboratory analysis.

WHY RECORD?

There is a marked division of opinion about the merits of sediment field recording systems, a point which was apparent at the 'Sediments in

Archaeology' symposium held at Southampton University, December 15–16, 1973 (Davidson and Shackley, 1975). One school of thought believed that it was essential to record the selection of relevant sediment characteristics which was thought *at the time of the excavation* to give the maximum potential information yield, and the other school argued that this was useless, since the information recorded would already be obsolete by the time that the excavation finished, because the questions to be asked would have changed. The writer holds the former opinion.

However, it is always difficult to decide what sediment characteristics to record, just as it is difficult to judge when a sample is needed. The recording criteria will vary with the nature of the site, the sets of problems posed and the competence of the operator, as well as with the anticipated use of the results. General remarks about the sediments are usually recorded in the site notebooks kept by excavation supervisors, and for this reason are seldom standardised even for one particular site. This lack of objectivity can be overcome to a certain extent by the use of printed forms or record cards, since it is easier to remember to note the presence or absence of a particular feature if all that is required is a tick on a card and a supplementary note. Each stratum can be recorded on this basis (Fedele, 1975). Various manuals have been produced for standardising field notes, the most useful being that published by the Soil Survey of Great Britain (1960), soon to be superseded by a new edition (Avery, 1974). This contains a methodology for recording a soil profile, which can usefully be adapted for the qualitative recording of an archaeological sediment sequence.

General information to be noted includes the precise position, site name, grid reference and locality, which can be printed on to a standard form. The date, feature or stratum number and the identity of the operator are always required, together with the shape and dimensions of the layer under consideration and its main characteristics. The nature and mode of formation should be recorded, and a description of the sediment texture. Several of the chemical tests described on p. 80 may also be used in the field.

SEDIMENT DESCRIPTIONS

A sediment type is a function of both the mineral constituents and the way that these are arranged in the sediment. The term *'texture'* is frequently used to describe a particular sediment type, although correctly it refers only to its predominant grain size. Although this cannot be accurately determined without a particle size analysis (p. 87), there are field tests which rely on the 'feel' of the sediment, obtained by working a small moist sample between the fingers and hand. The properties of the different size grades which compose the sediment can be described as follows:

(a) *Sand.* A loose and clean-grained material, of grain size $4–0.5\,\phi$. If a dry sample is squeezed in the hand, it will fall apart when the pressure is released. Coarse sand (grain diameter $1–0.5\,\phi$) has grains which 'grate' against each other in the hand sample, and which can easily be detected visually. In fine sand this effect is much less obvious, but the individual grains should still be distinguishable.

(b) *Silt*. Silt is finer-textured than sand and has rather a 'silky' feel. It may be slightly gritty, but the individual grains will not be distinguishable without the aid of a hand lens. The sediment will form a 'sludge' when wet.

(c) *Clay*. A clay forms hard lumps or clods when dry, but when moist is sticky, cohesive and plastic. It will form excellent casts, and has a grain diameter less than 8 ϕ.

The presence of a great deal of organic matter in a sediment tends to make it feel more clay-rich, and the presence of much calcium carbonate, as in very chalky deposits, imitates the feel of silt. It is rare to find sediments composed entirely of sand, silt or clay, rather than combinations of the three in different proportions.

(d) *Sandy loam*. A sediment which contains mostly sand but has enough silt and clay to make it cohesive. It will form a cast when moist, but the cast is easily broken. A true sandy loam contains 50% sand, 30% silt and 20% clay.

(e) *Loam*. Loam feels rather gritty in the hand, but has a reasonably smooth texture and is rather plastic. The moist sediment will form a good cast, and is composed of nearly equal parts of silt and sand, with about half their amounts of clay.

(f) *Silt loam*. This has a slightly silky feel, and will form clods when dry. The lumps are easily broken, the resulting material being rather soft and floury. Wet silt loam will form a thick 'sludge' and make good casts. It contains at least 50% of sand and silt together with 12–25% clay.

(g) *Clay loam*. A clay loam is a fine-textured deposit which will readily break up into clods or lumps that are hard when dry. The moist sediment is plastic and cohesive, and contains nearly equal amounts of sand and clay.

The individual grains are bound together to form a sediment, the strengths of the bond being described as the *coherence* of the material.

A   Moist sediments

0 = non-coherent
1 = very friable (crumbles under gentle pressure)
2 = friable (crumbles under moderate pressure)
3 = firm (crumbles under moderate pressure, with noticeable resistance)
4 = very firm (crumbles under strong pressure but is difficult to crush between the fingers)
5 = extremely firm (crumbles only under very strong pressure and must be broken apart bit by bit)

B   Dry sediments

0 = loose (non-coherent)
1 = soft (weakly coherent and fragile, breaks under light pressure)
2 = slightly hard (weakly resistant to pressure and easily broken between thumb and fingers)

3 = hard (resistant to pressure. Can be broken in the hand but difficult to break between thumb and forefinger)
4 = very hard (only broken in the hand with difficulty)
5 = extremely hard (cannot be broken in the hand)

The cementation of a sediment is a measure of the degree to which the grains have been chemically bound together by some substance other than clay minerals—for example, calcium carbonate, silica or iron oxides. The cementation of a sediment will be little affected by moistening. Some sediments can be so firmly cemented that they require fracturing with a geological hammer and rock chisels to sample, particularly iron or manganese pans or very hard cave breccias.

(a) *Weakly cemented* (brittle and hard but can be broken in the hand)
(b) *Strongly cemented* (brittle but cannot be broken in the hand)
(c) *Very strongly cemented* (will require a strong hammer blow to break)

COLOUR

Variations in natural sediment colour are often extremely significant and may be a valuable aid to description (Cornwall, 1958). Colour should be described by reference to a standard soil colour chart, preferably the Munsell system of soil colour notation. A set of Munsell charts should form part of the standard equipment for any field work or laboratory description of sediments. The use of standard charts eliminates the subjective verbal colour descriptions ('mouse-brown', 'medium-red') which mean different things to different people. Munsell charts are produced in loose-leaf folders, each chart with a plastics cover for protection[1]*. The reading of a soil colour is taken by comparing the sample (held on the end of a clean spatula) with the colour chips in the charts, and reading the notation of the chip nearest in colour to the soil. Other varieties of soil colour charts are manufactured, but these are not as reliable or as widely used.

The Munsell system recognises three attributes of colour—the *hue*, the *value* (degree of lightness or darkness) and the *chroma* (the degree of departure of a given hue from a neutral grey of the same colour). Each page in the charts contains a series of chips of different hues, with the value variations expressed on the vertical axis and the chroma variations along the horizontal (*Figure 2.1*). When the chip nearest in colour to the sample is located, the number is noted by first recording the hue (top of the card) and then the value and chroma, giving a format such as 7.5YR 2/6, or 2Y8/3. Each chip has a corresponding verbal description on the other side of the page.

Several points should be borne in mind when Munsell charts are used:

(a) All colours should be measured in daylight, preferably at the same time of day to eliminate errors due to light variations.

* Superior numbers in parentheses refer to the manufacturers listed in the Appendix.

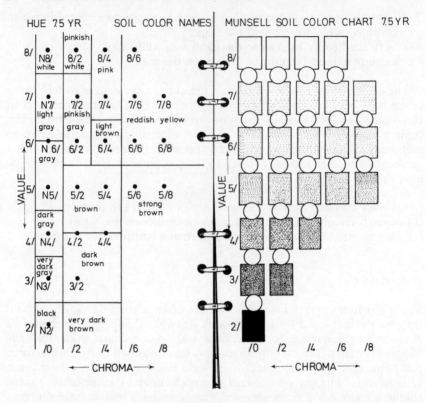

Fig. 2.1. Structure of a specimen page (hue 7.5YR) of a Munsell soil colour chart. The colour chips on the right-hand page correspond to descriptions on the left. (Courtesy Munsell Colour Division)

(b) All colours should ideally be recorded by the same person, since colour perception varies between individuals.

(c) Colour should be recorded from a freshly cleaned face and smeared surfaces avoided.

(d) The colour of a sediment may not be uniform. In this case the variations should be noted and the size of mottlings or shadings.

GRAIN ORIENTATION

The study of the relationships between the different grain units that compose a sediment is referred to as petrofabric analysis, and includes a consideration of the movements or forces that produced these relationships (e.g. the depositional environment or diagenetic changes). Particles that have been deposited in a moving medium tend to orientate themselves with their longest (a) axis parallel to the direction of flow, and the shortest (c) axis transverse to it. This fact has long been used in studies concerning the depositional history of sediments—for example, in glacial tills (West and

Donner, 1956), aeolian silts (Sen and Mukherjee, 1972) and the orientation of particles in running water (Johannson, 1963).

Grain orientation analysis is usually combined with a description of particle shape, sphericity and roundness (p. 44), and if the deposit is coarse-grained, with direct measurement of particle size. The following method is suitable for measuring the orientation of large pebbles in the field:

(1) Clean the site face. If only the orientation of the coarse material is of any interest, then the removal of finer sediment from the interstices is permissible, if this can be done without disturbing the pebbles.

(2) Mark the directions of the longest (a) and shortest (c) axes on the pebbles, using chalk or a spirit pen and a ruler. Measure these dimensions and record them on a standard sheet. It may be necessary to move the pebbles slightly for this, but great care must be taken to replace them exactly in their original positions.

(3) Measure the inclination of each pebble from the horizontal, by marking a horizontal line on the pebble with a spirit level and measuring the declination of the a and c axes with an inclinometer. The orientations of the axes (azimuths) are then recorded with a prismatic compass, by sighting along the measured lines.

Krumbein (1939) describes a method for three-dimensional plotting of the long (a) axis of pebbles using a small frame (5 × 6 in) with thin brass cross-wires and an attached spirit level. This is useful if a large number of orientation analyses have to be undertaken, and is very easy to construct. There is an equally simple method for making measurements from a photograph, which must be taken with the camera axis perpendicular to the surface being measured. This has the advantage of providing a permanent record and may be convenient if there is limited available time.

If a sample of material must be removed for measurement in the laboratory, the particles have to be consolidated *in situ*, using shellac, epoxy resins or clear plastics. Location, orientation and identity marks should clearly be marked on the specimen, and a photographic record and sketch map made. The clear plastics 'Quentsplass' range is particularly suitable for consolidation and is strong enough to hold quite large pebbles. The writer has used plastics impregnation successfully for taking undisturbed samples from sandy gravels. When the block sample arrives back in the laboratory, it must be cut along a plane parallel to any bedding to make the orientation measurements. If a thin section is required of a fine material, this must be taken and orientated with great care. Curray (1956) describes a suitable method for making grain orientation measurements in thin section using a projection microscope. Measurements can also be made using a radial reticule with 10° or 20° rays, inserted in the microscope eyepiece. The grains to be measured are sighted in the centre of the crossed hairs and the direction of the long (a) axis is measured. Several of the automated image analysers (p. 139) have facilities for grain orientation analysis, either in a hand sample or from a thin section.

The inclination and orientation of the particles are expressed by plotting them on a stereographic net. The polar equi-area net of Phillips (1960) is shown in *Figure 2.2* and has a centre point representing a pole at right angles to the plane of projection, with concentric circles for angular declinations from this pole at 10° intervals. The radial rays represent the azimuths. A horizontal particle would therefore lie at the outside of the

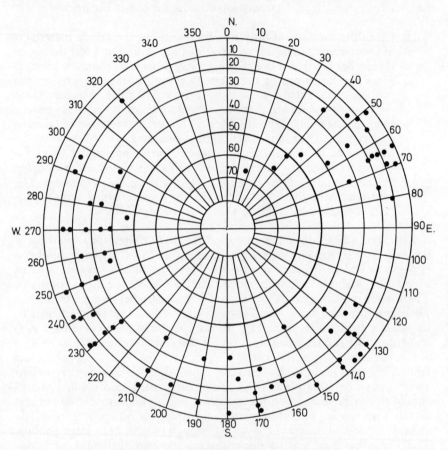

• = Danebury flint nodule *a* axis

Fig. 2.2. A polar equi-area stereographic net for plotting grain orientation measurements. The centre point represents a pole at right angles to the plane of projection, with concentric circles representing angular declinations at 10° intervals. The radial rays show the azimuths. The net has been completed with points taken from measurements on the Danebury flint pavement (after Phillips, 1960)

circle and could theoretically be shown by two dots 180° apart, but the plotting and contouring method recommended by Phillips takes this apparent anomaly into account.

Figure 2.2 shows the net completed with data points obtained from the analysis of an accumulation of large flints at the inner side of the rampart of the Iron Age hillfort of Danebury, Hampshire (*Figure 2.3*). The flints occurred within the occupation area and the excavator wondered whether or not they represented tumble from the rampart structure. Since the whole group was rather compacted, it was possible that they could have been deliberately placed there to serve as the foundation for some structure. If the material represented rampart tumble, a preferred orientation should be seen, whereas a deliberate packing of flint blocks would tend to be

Fig. 2.3. Chalk-cut pits at the Iron Age hillfort of Danebury, Hants. A view of the 1973 excavation, showing the complex of pits and post holes in the interior. The flint packing was found at the foot of the inner rampart, roughly aligned along the far edge of the excavation area.

randomly orientated. The lengths of the three axes of a representative sample of pebbles were measured, with their inclinations from the horizontal and their azimuths. The axial measurements were left as histograms and the other results plotted on the net. The dot scatter on a projected net is difficult to interpret visually, and it is usual to make a contour diagram of the points. This is done by estimating the percentage of dots per unit area of the surface of the net. A convenient way is to cut a hole of radius 1 cm in a piece of thin plastics or hard cardboard, and then to draw the net and plot the points on tracing paper, positioning it over a piece of metric graph paper. The cut circle is then moved over the net at each of the line intersections on the graph paper, and the numbers of dots appearing within it at each position are noted and expressed as percentages of the total. After the entire net has been covered in this way, the units are joined up at suitable (usually 1%) contour intervals.

Figure 2.4 shows the contour diagram for the Danebury flint tumble prepared using this principle. The angle of dip of the *a* axes can be seen

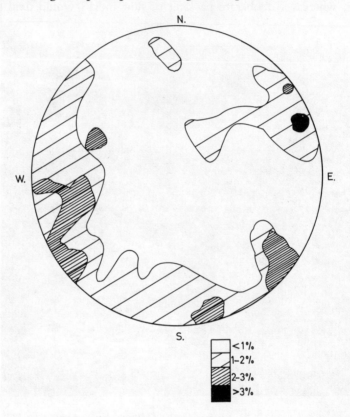

Fig. 2.4. Contour diagram for expressing grain orientation measurements. Completed with the same points as Fig. 2.2

to be rather low. There are two preferred orientations, as indicated by the contours, one following a line corresponding approximately to the transverse ground slope and the other, major mode, corresponding to the direction that should have been followed had the material tumbled from the rampart (approximately N E./S W.). This indicates the origin of the material, since had the packing been deliberate the orientation would have been random. The method is particularly suitable for linear or tabular rocks, but its accuracy decreases with increased sphericity and roundness.

INFORMATION STORAGE

DRAWINGS AND PHOTOGRAPHS

It may be necessary to draw or photograph the section in addition to recording numerical or verbal information. If the deposit is part of a site stratigraphy, then it will normally already have been drawn for archaeological purposes, but this drawing may need annotating. The writer has often found differences between the boundaries of a sediment stratum observed in the field and those recorded by the archaeological draughtsman. In addition there is little standardisation of drawing techniques and the conventions observed on a particular site—for example, in representing sediment compaction—may not be especially useful. White (1971) describes a suitable technique for sediment drawing.

Photographing sediment sections always presents problems, since it is very difficult to bring out contrasts between particular layers using standard techniques. Direct sunlight should always be avoided and discreet spraying may be required. A yellow–green filter may often help to distinguish layers, and a wide-angle lens is useful for photographing awkward sections. Extension rings or special 'macro' lenses can be added to the camera for very close work. A little judicious undercutting to highlight certain features may be done if the excavator permits it. White and Hayes (1961) discuss the use of stereo-colour photographs to record various types of soils, and recommend the use of an Ektachrome colour reversal film using flash attachments and the appropriate filters. Brongers (1966) discusses a special technique for photographing soil silhouettes with ultra-violet light. If any uncremated bone is present in the deposit, it will fluoresce and show on the print. This type of specialised technique is discussed further by Conlon (1973) and Cookson (1959).

INFORMATION STORAGE TECHNIQUES

The storage of basic archaeological information is best done by use of a computer, which provides both a permanent record and easy retrieval. All the card index systems in the world are fallible and destructible, but a permanent data storage system on magnetic tape or disc will last virtually for ever. Obviously the computer can best be used for storing verbal or numerical data, although current trends in computer graphics make the storage of diagrams, plans and charts a likely development in the future. Since quantitative sediment information principally consists of statistics and number sequences, computer-based storage is particularly suitable and is already a standard geological technique. In a previous paper (Shackley, 1973) the writer has advocated the use of a computer in archaeological sedimentology at three different levels. First, it may be used simply for data storage and retrieval systems—either on-site, using a remote terminal (Wilcock, 1973), or in the laboratory, using more conventional methods. Additional data obtained from laboratory analysis may be added at the same time, ideally combined in the same system with archaeological data. At a second level the computer may be used for basic data manipulations, the calculation of statistics and simple mathematical tests, together with graphical or diagrammatic presentation of results. The third operating level involves comparatively sophisticated data manipulations, which could not reasonably be attempted by 'hand' methods or with a desk calculator. These include techniques such as matrix analysis, multi-dimensional scaling, cluster analysis, discriminant analysis and seriation, which have already been applied to other branches of archaeology (Clark, 1973). The correlation and regression tests and other tests of the significance of sedimentological quantifications such as grain size parameters (p. 102) also come under this heading.

A flexible computer-based storage and retrieval system is surely essential for on-site sediment recording, and the PLUTARCH system, recently developed by Wilcock (Wilcock, 1974), is ideally suited to this purpose. The system was used for a pilot scheme during the 1973 excavation season at the Iron Age hillfort of Danebury (Stockbridge, Hants.). This site was intensively occupied from the fifth century B.C. until the Roman conquest, the defensive earthworks and massive gates encircling timber-built houses. All phases of the occupation are accompanied by numerous chalk cut pits (*Figure 2.3*), over 500 of which have already been excavated, and it is estimated that the total excavation of the site, planned to last for at least the next 5 years, will yield a sample of perhaps 5000 more. The majority of the pits were dug initially for storage, and after abandonment were either filled with rubbish or allowed to silt naturally with chalk weathering products. Each pit contains up to 15 distinct sedimentation layers, with large quantities of included archaeological and faunal material. It was decided to design and implement a computer-based recording system for these pit silts, recording information in the field directly on to computer coding sheets and adding other items of environmental and archaeological information afterwards in the laboratory. The handling and retrieval system used was PLUTARCH. The pilot recording scheme was sufficiently successful to warrant its adoption for the whole set of future excavation records, so that the information and recording system for both archaeological and environmental matters will now be computer-based. Field recording in the future will take place on to duplicated input sheets, one set of which will be kept by the excavator for immediate reference, the other set being sent away for data transference on to punched cards and submission to the computer (Shackley, 1975; Wilcock and Shackley, 1974).

At least 20 computer punch cards were required to record general information concerning each pit, including its dimensions, base angle, wall slope and contents. A further 16 cards were then used for each individual sediment layer within the pit, recording detailed characteristics of sediment texture and contents, including a simple coding system for sediment types. The dimensions of each layer were noted, together with the nature of its boundary and relationships to other layers. The whole system will be put on a firm chronological basis when the accurate typological sequence of pottery from each level has been completed, which will then be added to the computer records.

The system will provide a great deal of detailed information about the evolution of the site, and can be used to test hypotheses concerning the relationship between pit size and function, and the correlations of pit varieties with time. Observations can be made about recurring sedimentation patterns, and direct comparison of the characteristics of different layers and pits is facilitated. Sedimentological information includes a detailed record of the chalk weathering products sequence, including their accumulation rates and the differential preservation of organic material within them. The computer graphic facilities of PLUTARCH will be used to produce histograms and other diagrams of the various measured parameters, and to provide maps of the evolution of the site at different periods. The system is extremely flexible and data can be added or changed at later dates, since recall requirements will vary during a long-term project. The project will yield integrated information vital to the interpretation of such a large and complex site. It will also provide a model for future similar recording systems.

Although this approach is being applied here to a site with a comparatively closely defined series of problems, and where there is no surface stratigraphy, there seems no reason why similar approaches should not be valuable for the storage and processing of data from quite different types of site. Problems might arise with extremely complex urban sequences, but records of cave sites or excavations with comparatively easily interpreted stratigraphic relationships should respond well to this type of approach. Laflin (1974) has designed a system particularly suitable for rescue excavation, where time is often limited and records are not always of optimum accuracy. If a computerised recording scheme is to become common practice in future excavations, there seems little reason why the results of environmental studies and other 'specialist' fields should not be integrated with archaeological data right from the start, and indeed this would seem to be only logical. The chief requirement of the retrieval and storage systems is that they must be flexible, since it will often be necessary to add or modify data after the excavation. Since all laboratory work is time-consuming, the more accurate and standardised the site recording the less laboratory work will be required, except in cases where a particular problem requires a sophisticated analytical technique. With the advent of site sieving to recover molluscan remains and small animal bones, and flotation techniques for plant remains, the whole approach to excavation is taking on a multidisciplinary flavour, and the integration of the results of this work at the site level is obviously desirable.

References

AVERY, B. W. (1974). *Soil Survey Laboratory Methods* (Soil Survey Technical Monograph No. 6, Soil Survey of England and Wales)
BRONGERS, A. (1966). 'Ultra violet fluorescence photography of a soil silhouette of an interred corpse,' *Ber. Rijksdienst Oudheidkundig Bodemonderzoek*, **15–16**, 227–228

CLARK, D. L. (1973). *Analytical Archaeology* (Thames and Hudson, London)

CONLON, V. M. (1973). *Camera Techniques in Archaeology* (John Baker, London)

COOKSON, M. B. (1959). *Photography for Archaeologists* (John Baker, London)

CORNWALL, I. W. (1958). *Soils for the Archaeologist* (Phoenix, London)

CURRAY, J. R. (1956). 'Dimensional grain orientation studies of Recent coastal sands', *Bull. Am. Assoc. Petrol. Geologists*, **40**, 2440–2456

DAVIDSON, D. A. and SHACKLEY, M. L. (eds.) (1975). *Geoarchaeology: Earth Science and the Past* (Duckworth, London)

FEDELE, F. (1975). 'Sediments as palaeo–land segments', in *Geoarchaeology: Earth Science and the Past*, ed. Davidson, D. A. and Shackley, M. L. (Duckworth, London)

JOHANNSSON, C. A. (1963). 'Orientation of pebbles in running water', *Geografiska Annaler*, **XLV** (2–3), 85–112

KRUMBEIN, W. C. (1939). 'Preferred orientation of pebbles in sedimentary deposits', *Journal of Geology*, **47**, 673–706

LAFLIN, S. (1974). 'A recording scheme for excavations', *Computer Applications in Archaeology*, **2**, 71–75

PHILLIPS, F. C. (1960). *The Use of Stereographic Projection in Structural Geology* (Arnold, London)

SEN, R. and MUKERJEE, A. D. (1972). 'The relationship of petrofabrics with directional orientations of mineral grains from soil parent materials', *Soil Science*, **113**, 57–59

SHACKLEY, M. L. (1973). 'Computers and sediment analysis in archaeology', *Science in Archaeology*, **9**, 29–30

SHACKLEY, M. L. (1975). 'The Danebury project: an experiment in site sediment recording', in *Geoarchaeology: Earth Science and the Past*, ed. Davidson, D. A. and Shackley, M. L. (Duckworth, London)

SOIL SURVEY OF GREAT BRITAIN (1960). *Field Description of Soil Profiles*

WEST, R. G. and DONNER, D. J. (1956). 'East Anglian Tills, orientation analysis', *Quarterly Journal of the Geological Society*, **112**, 69

WHITE, L. P. (1971). 'A new technique for soil pit illustration', *Journal of Soil Science*, **23**, 58–61

WHITE, E. E. and HAYES, R. J. (1961). 'The use of stereo-colour photography for soil profile studies', *Photographic Journal*, **101**, 211–215

WILCOCK, J. D. (1973). 'The use of remote terminals for archaeological site records', *Computer Applications in Archaeology*, **1**, 64–69

WILCOCK, J. D. (1974). 'The "PLUTARCH" system', *Computer Applications in Archaeology*, **2**

WILCOCK, J. D. and SHACKLEY, M. L. (1974). 'The recovery of information from Iron Age pits: The Danebury project and PLUTARCH', *Computer Applications in Archaeology*, **2**, 82–90

Chapter 3

TAKING SAMPLES

SAMPLING THEORY

All laboratory work relies heavily on sampling experiments as sources of information. It is impossible to analyse the whole of a stratum and a comparatively small portion has therefore to be used as a sample. The problem is to make this small amount representative of the whole (Rootenberg, 1964). Since those who may read the results of the analysis and use them in further interpretation of the site will, in general, not know the sampling procedure that was undertaken, it is the responsibility of the *analyst* to ensure that his sample is truly representative of the parent material, and that it was taken with care and with a specific problem in mind. A properly taken sample is selected from a population in such a way that statistical theory is applicable (Binford, 1964; Krumbein, 1965; Heitzer, 1959; Cowgill, 1964). In addition, the size of the sample needs to be large enough to permit of satisfactory conclusions about the problem being studied.

RANDOM SAMPLING

The process of random sampling is often misunderstood, and many non-scientists mistakenly believe that a random sample is one that is taken without any *conscious* bias on the part of the operator (Cochran, 1963). This may lead to sampling procedures equivalent to blindfolding the sampler and pointing him, and his trowel, in the general direction of the area to be sampled. The elimination of conscious bias, which manifests itself in, for example, taking a sample only from the most accessible part of the section, or in choosing a portion that does not contain inconveniently large pebbles, still does not ensure that the resultant sample is fully representative of its parent population.

A *representative sample* is a selection of individual elements from a population in the exact proportion in which they exist in the original population. This representative sample must be random. A *random sample* is taken to estimate a representative sample of a population of unknown composition. The larger the random sample the greater the probability that it resembles

23

a truly representative sample. All laboratory treatment of archaeological sediments is based on the assumption that a true random sample is present, and if this is so then any one item, parameter or characteristic in the original population is as likely to be represented in the sample as any other, and the collection is free from conscious or unconscious bias. However, it is almost impossible to fully eliminate conscious bias, and quite impossible to eliminate unconscious bias unless a standard procedure of sample selection is undertaken.

When a sample is taken it is important to know the reason for sampling, since this affects both sample size and sampling plan. For example, if a series of calcareous ditch silts are being sampled for molluscan remains, closely spaced samples or a monolith are recommended, whereas samples taken to establish the sedimentary processes responsible for the sequence can be taken from the individual layers at wider intervals. The sample size required for insect remains may be several hundred times the size required by a pollen analyst.

SAMPLING TECHNIQUES

SAMPLING FROM AN OPEN SECTION

The samples taken will generally be of three types: a 'grab' sample of a fixed volume from within a relatively small area of an exposure, a 'channel' sample taken from an elongated strip extended into the interior of the section, or a series of stratified samples. The sample size required is directly proportional to the coarseness of the material and to the tests required. *Table 3.1* lists the minimum required sample weights for different particle

Table 3.1   APPROXIMATE SAMPLE SIZES REQUIRED FOR ACCURATE PARTICLE SIZE ANALYSIS OF SEDIMENTS

Particle diameter (mm)	Minimum weight required (kg)
64	50
50	35
40	15
25	5
20	2
12.5	1
10	0.5
5	0.2

sizes (Mace, 1964). The values here are calculated on the hypothesis that a particle size distribution is required.

For sediments with average particle sizes of less than 5 mm a sample of standard size, generally 1 kg, is taken, except for very fine material such as clay, where a much smaller sample is required. It must also be remembered that if tests additional to the particle size analysis are proposed, the initial bulk sample must be larger. It is often necessary to split the bulk sample into smaller fractions in the laboratory (p. 35), a procedure preferable to taking a series of small sub-samples in the field, since if these are taken from slightly different locations their composition may be different. Exceptions to this rule must of course be made if a sample for some specific purpose (perhaps radiocarbon dating) is required, in addition to the standard laboratory sample. *Table 3.1* illustrates the fact that very large sample sizes are theoretically required if the deposit is very coarse, and it is often simpler to carry out description and analysis of coarse deposits in the field wherever possible (p. 42).

The first step in sampling an open section is to clean the section face thoroughly. If a completely vertical section is not available, or the depth of material is too great, the face may have to be 'stepped', in which case the sampling points must be recorded with even greater care than usual. Sections from which sediment samples are taken should be drawn and photographed, and the precise sampling locations marked. If a vertical series of samples is to be taken, this must be done from the base of the section upwards, to avoid contamination. Samples taken from a horizontal area require the same type of precautions, including the cleaning of the exposure to a depth of several centimetres, if possible, to minimise the possibility of contamination.

Samples of very compacted material should be placed in thick, heavy-duty plastics bags, more than one layer of bag being used to prevent punctures due to protruding edges. A supply of 2 kg capacity bags, large potato-sacks and small self-sealing 'Minigrip'[5] bags should be readily available. It is wise to carry a supply of ready-cut string and labels, since this saves time and is helpful if samples are being taken in adverse lighting or otherwise poor conditions (for example, at the bottom of a damp cave). Bags should be tightly sealed with string and labelled with plastics tabs written on with waterproof ink. If more than one layer of bag is used, an additional label should be placed between the bags. The necks of plastics sample bags should never be knotted, since they become difficult to undo and this wastes time. *Never* place a label inside a bag containing sediment which might conceivably require chemical analysis, since the ink may cause contamination. It is inadvisable to label samples in pencil or ball-point; waterproof spirit inks or permanent markers are preferable. The use of cardboard or paper labels is to be discouraged. Samples should never be taken in paper bags or boxes, although small samples may be taken perfectly adequately in glass or plastics bottles or tubes. The label on the sample bag should record the number of the sample and its exact location, together with the reason for taking the sample, a grid reference, the site name and the name of the analyst. Fuller details should be set out in a sampling notebook. The use of a sample record notebook is a step that is often omitted from archaeological records, and it is common to find sediment sample locations mixed in with small-find notes in general site records, if indeed they are kept at all. If the correct procedure is followed and the samples are taken by the analyst who is destined to receive them, or at least under his supervision, then the problem is overcome, since he will have his own recording system. *Figure 3.1* illustrates the lay-out of a suitable sample record notebook, which

26

Site name	Feature No. etc.	Sample grid ref.	Sampling-plan	Reason for sampling	Sample identification No.	Date	Field treat-ment?	Sample description
Danebury	*PF 435-8*	*J. 247039*	*Series of samples from each layer*	*Basal layer ? contained charcoal*	*DAN / 435-8*	*5.3.73*	*none*	*grey silt with chalk*

Fig. 3.1. Suggested lay-out of a sample record book

may conveniently occupy a double-page spread in a hardback manilla book, or else be recorded straight on to computer input coding sheets (p. 20), or filed with a laboratory worksheet.

SAMPLING EQUIPMENT

EQUIPMENT FOR SAMPLING CEMENTED SEDIMENTS (for example, cave breccias)

(a) Geological hammer (2–3 lb head, wooden handle)[6]
(b) Prismatic compass
(c) Hand lens ($\times$ 10 magnification)
(d) Inclinometer[2]
(e) Brightly coloured field notebook or other recording system. Waterproof pen, labels, string, sampling bags
(f) Trowel
(g) Steel tape (3 m)
(h) Spatula and field knife
(i) Camera, capable of close focusing, and a small photographic scale
(j) If the rock is very hard, a small one-handed sledge[6] may be required (18 in long with a 2–3 lb head), and some small steel rock chisels.

EQUIPMENT FOR SAMPLING UNCONSOLIDATED SEDIMENTS

This was discussed at length by Sohl (1965). The hammer, chisels and sledge mentioned above will not be required, but the other equipment will be necessary, together with a set of large plastics spoons, several spatulas and forceps, and some kitchen roll for cleaning them between samples.

TAKING A MONOLITH

Sampling from an open section with a monolith tin[2] is an excellent method for ensuring that the sediment arrives back at the laboratory relatively undisturbed, and is particularly suitable for very fine sediments, such as laminated silts and clays, and for sampling through soil profiles. The monolith may later be divided to obtain the required analytical samples. The monolith tin, preferably of aluminium, lined with a plastics sheet, is hammered into the cleaned face. The tin needs to be about 50 cm long, 15 cm wide and 15 cm deep, as larger sizes become too heavy and difficult to transport. The plastics lining aids extraction of the material in the laboratory. After the monolith has been obtained, the top and bottom and precise sampling location should be written on the tin with a spirit pen, and the tin then sealed with aluminium foil and placed in a large heavy-duty plastics bag for transport. The method is not recommended for sampling coarse materials or unconsolidated sands.

SAMPLING BY CORING

A core sample should never be used for laboratory analysis unless this is unavoidable, since it is much easier to get an undisturbed and representative sample from an open face. An *auger* may be useful for tasks such as locating bedrock or indicating subsoil types, but is not a reliable method of obtaining samples. The single-spiral auger[2] is preferred, if it must be used, since this causes marginally less distortion than the double-spiral variety. It can be driven in by hand to a depth of several metres, by use of extension tubes and considerable force. The difficulty of augering increases proportionally with depth and sediment compaction, and more than one person may often be needed. Samples will always be distorted, and often contaminated by the passage through surface layers during the process of removal. If the sediment is wet, or if there is a soft layer covered by a harder one, the sample will ooze or be squeezed out of the auger by pressure before it can reach the surface. Many varieties of screw, bucket and posthole augers are manufactured, but they are all subject to the same disadvantages. Several alternatives to the auger are also manufactured, which are principally used for sampling organic sediments. These are discussed by West (1968), Faegri and Iversen (1965) and Wright, Livingstone and Cushing (1965), and are principally divisible into the hand-operated samplers attached to a series of rigid rods and the heavier sampling devices of commercial pattern that are favoured by engineering and constructional workers for obtaining rather large cores. These latter devices often require specialised rigs and vehicles, and are expensive. Bearing in mind the limitations inherent in core sampling if any accuracy in analysis is required, it is doubtful whether the use of such rigs is ever fully justifiable.

Table 3.2   HAND-OPERATED SAMPLING DEVICES (AFTER WEST, 1968)

Type	Sample length (cm)	width (cm)	Deformation of sediment	Compression of sediment	Suitability
Augers					
Screw auger	25	4	Much	Little	Compacted organic sediment clay and silt
Other augers	10–30	5–10	Much	Little	As above + sand and gravel
Samplers					
Hiller peat borer	50	3	Much	None	Peat or compact mud
Russian peat borer	50	5	None	None	Peat or mud
Livingstone borer	50	4	Little	Some	Non-fibrous peat, mud
Punch sampler	50	6	Little	Some	Compact organic sediment clay, silt and sand

Several of the hand-operated samplers are useful, notably the *Hiller sampler* for mud or very compacted silts, which will provide a 50-cm-long core, rather distorted. The *Russian peat borer* enables a sample of similar size to be obtained and causes rather less distortion (Gray, 1965). *Table 3.2* presents the advantages and disadvantages of various hand-operated samplers.

PRESERVING THE SURFACE LAYERS OF A SECTION

There are several methods available by which the thin surface layers of a vertical or horizontal section may be preserved, by 'peeling' off the surface material to obtain a thin sheet which is then backed and transported to the laboratory. This idea does not, of course, produce an analytical sample, but is an excellent way of preserving and recording a stratigraphic series and presenting the results in a permanent and spectacular manner. The techniques involved have generally been used by excavators desiring this type of visual presentation for some specific purpose, since an equivalent result can be achieved by suitably detailed drawings, photographs and samples.

CELLULOID AND ACETATE 'PEELS'

Franken (1965) describes the method that he used for consolidating a section through a *tell* sequence (Tell Deir'Alla) in the Jordan valley. This involved cleaning the area, preferably one about 50×50 cm square, and then rolling on a thin solution of celluloid and acetone, followed by three thicker coats. The chemicals are best sprayed on if the climate is not so hot that it causes the acetone to evaporate. A paper-thin pull-off is obtained, with a fine surface layer of particles adhering to the chemical film, which must then be mounted on a plywood backing. The method is both cheap and simple, but should only be used for very fine sediments, since the peel is so thin that it tears easily and will not hold larger pebbles very firmly. Repeated coats to increase thickness have the effect of making the whole sheet brittle.

'ARBORITE' CONTACT CEMENT

This method was also used at the above-mentioned site, and was considered by Franken (1965) to be superior to the celluloid–acetone peel. It involves the cleaning of the area followed by the application of two thick coats of commercial 'Arborite'. In the case of very crumbly sediments a thin coat of celluloid–acetone mixture may be applied underneath for consolidation. The resultant product is a rubbery sheet, sufficiently tough and flexible to retain lumpy objects and very difficult to pierce. A plastics sheet should be stuck on to the surface of the 'Arborite' before it dries, and after the 'peel' has been lifted surplus earth may be gently scraped away from the other side with a knife. The 'peel' is then again backed with plywood for transport. Approximately one tin (quart size) of 'Arborite' is required per square metre of section.

LACQUER 'PEELS'

West (1968) and Voigt (1949) describe a method for making 'peels' using polyvinyl acetate. The surface should be carefully cleaned and a nearly vertical section left. Ideally the sediment should be slightly moist. A horizontal gully is cut along the top of the section near the edge, and a 3:1 mixture of lacquer (PVA) and thinner (acetone) is poured in. This overflows down the section from the gully. More mixture is added until the whole section has been covered, which will require about 2 kg of the mixture per square metre of section. The lacquer may also be sprayed on. A more concentrated mixture is required for sands than for clays, and for very high sections. The lacquer should be left to dry for a day. West (1968) recommends that gauze be laid on the surface to strengthen it, and incorporated into the 'peel' by painting over with dilute lacquer. The 'peel' is then again backed with plywood or hardboard for transport. Thicker sections may be consolidated in this manner as well.

COMMERCIAL PLASTICS

The writer has experimented with several commercial plastics for hardening sections, the most suitable being the 'Quentsplass' range, designed as plastics floor-coatings[4]. These have the advantage of being moderately cheap, quick to harden and extremely tough. The drying time varies with the humidity, temperature and dilution of the plastics, but a sandy section will take approximately 5–6 h to dry on a warm English summer day. A further 24 h must elapse to allow complete hardening, but the section can be carefully removed to the laboratory in that time. The plastics may either be sprayed on to a cleaned vertical section, in a manner similar to that described for the 'Arborite', or can be used to consolidate small horizontal areas. The method is particularly useful for preserving interesting sedimentary structures or similar features intact.

SAMPLING ORGANIC SEDIMENTS

For pollen analysis. The section must be extra-carefully cleaned, and sampled from the base upwards. Samples of at least 1 cm^3 in size should be removed with a clean spatula, at 5 cm intervals, and stored in airtight plastics bags or glass tubes. If a monolith is taken (see p. 27) an aluminium tin should always be used, well sealed with aluminium foil and plastics sheet, or with paraffin wax. Great care must be taken to avoid contamination, either during sampling or during storage. Most palynologists will prefer to take their own samples, and this should, of course, be checked beforehand. Samples taken for pollen analysis are best stored in a deep freeze, although some writers recommend oven drying at 105 °C before storage (Faegri and Iversen, 1965).

For charcoals. If charcoal is to be collected for the identification of the species present, it needs to be packed very carefully, and it is pointless collecting all the small fragments of a large piece. Pack in small boxes lined with kitchen roll, and then in labelled plastics bags.

For grain and seeds. Large samples are required (at least 2 kg each), which must be stored in plastics bags inside cardboard boxes to minimise crushing during transport. Recent experiments have shown that the extraction of such material on site is preferable to sampling (Higgs, 1972).

For wood and other macroscopic plant remains. If the samples are not to be used for radiocarbon dating, they should be kept moist in a dilute solution of 'Carbowax' (polyethylene glycol)[3], in distilled water, in a plastics bag or glass receptacle.

For mollusca. A large bulk sample is again required, as for grain or seeds. Much preliminary work can be done on site by wet sieving (Evans, 1972). Samples should be taken in a stratified series.

For insect remains. Special care is required to ensure that fragile insect remains reach the laboratory intact. Pack very carefully, keeping moist if necessary, and avoid crushing. A very large bulk sample is required, 20–25 kg if possible.

For radiocarbon dating. Remove the sample with plastics tools, taking great care to avoid contamination. Seal immediately in airtight plastics bags and consult the manual published by the appropriate dating laboratory for their required treatment. These will vary with the different laboratories and with different sampling materials. If in doubt keep the sample airtight and leave it alone (Council for British Archaeology, 1970). If the sample is of plant material, twigs and leaves should be taken, not heartwood (Pollach and Golson, 1966).

References

BINFORD, L. (1964). 'A consideration of archaeological research design', *American Antiquity*, **29**, 425–441

COCHRAN, W. G. (1963). *Sampling Techniques* (Chapman and Hall, London)

COUNCIL FOR BRITISH ARCHAEOLOGY (1970). *Handbook of Scientific Aids and Evidence for Archaeologists* (London)

COWGILL, G. L. (1964). 'The selection of samples from large sherd collections', *American Antiquity*, **29**, 467–473

EVANS, J. G. (1972). *Land Snails in Archaeology* (Seminar Press, London)

FAEGRI, K. and IVERSEN, J. (1965). 'Field techniques', in *Handbook of Palaeontological Techniques*, ed. Kummel, B. and Raup, D. (Freeman, New York)

FRANKEN, H. J. (1965). 'Taking the baulks home', *Antiquity*, **39**, 140–142

GRAY, J. (1965). 'Palynological techniques', in *Handbook of Palaeontological Techniques*, ed. Kummel, B. and Raup, D. (Freeman, New York)

HEITZER, R. F. (1959). *The Archaeologist at Work: A Source Book in Archaeological Methods and Inter-pretation* (Harper and Row, New York)

HIGGS, E. S. (ed.) (1972). *Papers in Economic Prehistory* (Cambridge University Press)

KRUMBEIN, W. C. (1965). 'Sampling in palaeontology', in *Handbook of Palaeontological Techniques*, ed. Kummel, B. and Raup, D. (Freeman, New York)

MACE, A. E. (1964). *Sample Size Determination* (New York)

POLACH, H. A. and GOLSON, J. (1966). 'Collection of specimens for radiocarbon dating and inter-pretation of results', *Manual 2. Australian Institute of Aboriginal Studies*

ROOTENBERG, S. (1964). 'Archaeological field sampling', *American Antiquity*, **30**, 181–188

SOHL, N. F. (1965). 'Collecting in unconsolidated sediments', in *Handbook of Palaeontological Techniques*, ed. Kummel, B. and Raup, D. (Freeman, New York)

VOIGT, E. (1949). 'Die Anwendung der Lackfilm—Methode bei der Bergung geologischer und bodenkundlicher Profile', *Mitt. Geol. Staatsinst. Hamburg*, **19**, 111–129

WEST, R. G. (1968). *Pleistocene Geology and Biology* (Wiley, Chichester)

WRIGHT, H. E., LIVINGSTONE, D. A. and CUSHING, E. J. (1965). 'Coring devices for lake sediments' in *Handbook of Palaeontological Techniques*, cd. Kummel, B. and Raup, D. (Freeman, New York)

Chapter 4

THE PREPARATION OF SAMPLES FOR ANALYSIS

INITIAL PREPARATION

The sample should have reached the laboratory in sealed plastics bags, or in sample phials, but it will then require pre-treatment of some kind before analysis can begin. Before any treatment is begun, a detailed description of the sample should have been made, including remarks on the sampling method and plan used, and on the position of the sampling point in relation to drawn or photographed sections. A summary of this information should be kept on a standard record card, together with notes on the dimensions of the sample and any additional field details. The same card or sheet may conveniently be used to record the pre-treatment, and to act as an indicator for the required laboratory analyses. *Figure 4.1* shows a card suitable for this purpose.

This particular card records basic information about a sample taken from an early Medieval site at Wareham, Dorset. The excavator noted the distinctive character of the material and required a laboratory analysis to determine whether the sediment was likely to be a natural accumulation *in situ* or whether it could represent accumulated debris from a nearby hearth. The sample was examined under a stereomicroscope, and a series of chemical tests and a particle size analysis were done. The sediment proved to be rich in burnt flint, burnt quartz sand grains, burnt clay, wood charcoal and ash. Phosphate and humus values were high, and the material had a strongly alkaline pH value, in contrast to the surrounding material, which was derived from the local acid podsols. It was concluded that the material represented hearth debris.

DRYING

If the initial sample is damp, then it should be dried in an oven for several hours at 105–110 °C, care being taken that the original colour has been noted in the field, and any subsequent changes due to the drying process. Drying should never be undertaken if any biological material contained

33

in the sample is to be examined, as this will be affected by the application of heat. If the sample has a high clay content, the drying temperature must be lowered and the drying time extended, suitable values being 50 °C for 2–3 days. This prevents heavy 'caking'. During drying any contamination

Site	Sample No.	Exact location
WAREHAM (DORSET)	WAREHAM 21/3	*see section drawing*

Field record on section/notebook	Remarks *Dark grey-brown sand*
Sample sent by *P. Hinton*	....
Sample taken by ...."........	....
Pre-treatment done by *HS*	....
Analysis done by *MB*	Date *5-3-73*

LABORATORY DESCRIPTION

Colour *Munsell 10 YR 4.2 (dark greyish brown)*	Included archaeological/organic matter *Burnt flint and charcoal Burnt fragments of pottery*
Texture etc. *Mainly sand, silt & clay < 5 %*	Reason for analysis *? Derived from nearby hearth*

PRE-TREATMENT

Drying only required	✓	Organic matter removed	—
Weight of bulk sample	*592.34 gm*	Carbonates removed	—
Splitting method	*Rotary splitter*	Iron oxides removed	—
Weight(s) of sub-sample(s)	*12 x C. 60 gm*	Other pre-treatment (specify)	—
Weight of sample No. (1) after pre-treatment	*1-59.36 for particle size analysis*	*Two other subsamples required for chemical tests and visual description remaining 9 recombined*	

TESTS REQUIRED

Particle size analysis	✓	Grain shape description	—
Thin section	—	Heavy mineral analysis	—
Examination and description	✓	Chemical tests (specify)	*? Phosphates ? Humus*
Scanning electron microscope	—	Examination of organic material	*Check if present*
Other (specify)	—	Other (specify)	—

Fig. 4.1. Sample record sheet

from laboratory dust should be avoided and particular attention paid to avoid the confusion of sample labels in the drying oven. Drying is best carried out on steel or aluminium drying trays, labelled with a spirit pen and not with sticky labels, since these often become detached on heating.

SPLITTING

Field samples may often contain more material than is required for a laboratory analysis, and will therefore require subdividing. It is necessary to divide the sample in such a way that the original characteristics of the bulk sample are exactly represented in the sub-sample. Sediments may have become sorted during transport from the site, and concentrations of heavy minerals or large grains may have formed in the corners of the bag. Some form of remixing and splitting is therefore always recommended, even if the sample size does not need to be substantially reduced. It is, however, always wise to preserve a small fraction of the original sample which has not been analysed or treated, since some laboratory disaster or the development of a new technique may necessitate its use in later years. This fraction must truly represent the original sample. The writer recommends the collection and permanent storage of such a small sub-sample (in a large sealed glass phial) as part of the standard recording procedure.

Obtaining representative samples from the original bulk sample may be done by 'hand' methods, but some form of mechanical splitting is preferred, and ensures far greater accuracy.

'QUARTERING'

This is a simple and inaccurate method of dividing the sample by hand. It should never be used if accurate particle size or chemical analyses are planned, since the results obtained on sub-samples taken by this method may deviate by up to 20% from the ideal, owing to sampling errors. The method is generally used on fine-grained sandy materials of initial bulk weight 50–100 g.

(1) Heap the dry sample up into a cone, on a piece of filter paper.
(2) Cut the cone into quarters with a clean knife or thin metal sheet.
(3) Remove the first and third (or second and fourth) quarters with a clean spatula. Repeat stages (1) and (2) until a sub-sample of suitable size has been obtained.

RIFFLE BOXES

Riffle boxes are used to divide a large initial sample of fairly coarse material into two approximately equal parts. They consist of a metal frame with a series of slots (*Figure 4.2*), of different dimensions according to the approximate particle size of the material to be divided. They are especially suitable for coarse and medium-sized pebbles, although they may also be used for dry sand. The dry sediment is poured in at the top of the apparatus, in one smooth movement along the length of the box. This ensures that each particle has a theoretically equal chance of falling down any of the slots, which lead alternately into two metal boxes[2]. Care must be taken not to use the riffle box for particles of greater average size than its slot widths, since this results in particles becoming jammed, and they are then difficult to extract and bend the slots. The riffling procedure should be repeated until samples of the required size have been obtained. The method is more accurate than 'quartering', useful for coarser samples and less 'messy'. It is still liable to quite substantial sampling errors.

Brewer and Barrow (1972) describe a microsplitter which is particularly useful for obtaining very small samples for slide preparation.

ROTARY SAMPLE SPLITTERS

The first rotary sample splitters were developed in the 1930s, to enable unbiased sub-samples to be obtained from a heterogeneous main sample, on the principle that the delivery of a concentration of a particular component from a rotating feed hopper cannot, by any theory of probability, coincide cyclically with the passage of one particle receiver under the feed outlet. Several commercial firms manufacture rotary splitters on this principle, most of which are particularly suitable for fine material, especially sand. *Figure 4.3* shows the Swift Model 92 rotary sample splitter[7], which will give up to 12 sub-samples at once from an initial bulk sample. The collecting bins are stationary and a bulk sample of up to 1500 cm^3 can be processed, particle sizes up to 3 mm ($-1.5\,\phi$) being suitable for this model.

DISAGGREGATION

The dry sample may be gently crushed in the fingers or with a rubber pestle and mortar (*Figure 4.2*). Vigorous crushing should be avoided, since this removes natural as well as artificial grain aggregates and may also crush individual particles. If the sample is aggregated, then the percentage of aggregates must be noted, since it will affect the particle size distribution. Before analysis is attempted a few grams of the sample should be scattered on a filter paper and examined under a low-power binocular microscope (generally at $\times 10$ or $\times 20$ magnification), the aggregates and their sizes being noted on a micrometer scale (p. 137). The aggregate frequency can then be estimated.

A decision must be taken whether or not to remove carbonates, organic matter, iron oxides and other constituents of the sample, which will depend on the nature of the sample and the planned analysis. The procedure described below for the removal of organic matter with hydrogen peroxide may also be used for disaggregation, and for a pre-treatment before particle size analysis, since it has no effect on the composition of the silt–clay fraction.

Ultrasonic tanks are used in many laboratories for the cleaning of equipment, and they also provide a quick and effective method for sample disaggregation. Ultrasonics Ltd[8] manufacture a series of tanks of

Fig. 4.2. Riffle boxes and pestle and mortar for sample preparation

Fig. 4.3. The Swift rotary sample splitter. (Reproduced by courtesy of James Swift and Son Ltd)

internal diameter 5–20 in, which for this purpose should be filled with water. Electric energy from the apparatus generator is passed to the transducers, which convert it to sound energy that passes through the water. A suspension of fine sediment in a beaker is lowered into the tank for a few seconds, where the cavitation effect of the sound energy effectively disaggregates the grains. This procedure should not be used if a scanning electron microscope examination is planned, since it may affect the surface textures of the individual grains. It is an excellent pre-treatment for particle size analysis or chemical tests (Genrich and Bremner, 1972). Prolonged ultrasonic treatment is an effective dispersant for the most consolidated sediments.

REMOVAL OF FINE MATERIAL FROM A BULK SAMPLE, FOR PARTICLE SIZE ANALYSIS

If a bulk sample contains a great deal of silt and clay it will be impossible to process it by dry sieving, and any splitting method will be inaccurate. The following method is recommended for removing the fine fraction:

(1) Position a 63 μm sieve (4 ϕ) over a large beaker, taking care that it is resting on its rim, not its mesh.
(2) Place the sample on it a few grams at a time, and wash through the mesh with a gentle jet of water. Do not attempt to crush the material, or place a weight of any kind upon the sieve, since this will distort the mesh.
(3) After all the sample has been washed through, tip the coarse fraction (retained on the sieve) on to a drying tray, and oven dry for a few hours at 100 °C. Gently evaporate the fine fraction (less than 4 ϕ) in the beaker at about 50 °C, and store the resulting fine powder in an airtight sample phial.

If the sample is a large one and is composed of much material finer than sand, a set of larger-mesh sieves should be used in addition to the 4 ϕ sieve, at least two (1 ϕ and 3 ϕ) being positioned above the finer sieve. The material must be collected on these sieves and dried as in stage (3) above.

DISPERSION OF SUSPENDED SEDIMENTS

Deflocculating agents may be required for the particle size analysis of suspended sediments. The use of 'Calgon' (sodium hexametaphosphate) in 10% solution is recommended. A suitable volume is equal to $A \times B$, where A = weight of the sample and B = estimated percentage of clay. Alternatively, a fixed volume of 'Calgon' may be added, generally 1 ml 10% 'Calgon' per gram of estimated clay, or a constant 50 ml 'Calgon' for each 200–300 cm³ of sample. If too much 'Calgon' is used, it will reduce the accuracy of the analysis, and it may be necessary to flocculate with a chemical such as 'Polyox' or 'Magnafloc F140', or to recentrifuge, decant, wash and restart the experiment.

Other suitable dispersants include solutions of sodium tripolyphosphate, tetrasodium phosphate, sodium carbonate, sodium hydroxide or sodium oxalate. 'Calgon' remains the most efficient dispersant, since it does not precipitate insoluble calcium phosphate.

REMOVAL OF UNWANTED CONSTITUENTS

REMOVAL OF ORGANIC MATERIAL

Organic material may often constitute a significant sample contaminant, and in that case should be removed. It is not normally heavy enough to affect the particle size distribution if this is obtained by sieving, but it may bind together the constituent particles and reduce the accuracy of a sedimentation or microscopic analysis. Organic material should never be removed simply by burning it off the dry sample, since this causes fracturing of the sand grains and may fuse together clay particles and generally affect the mineral composition.

REMOVAL OF ORGANIC MATTER USING HYDROGEN PEROXIDE (H_2O_2)

This is the most suitable method, since hydrogen peroxide does not affect the clay mineral composition. It should not be used for pyritic sediments or those with much free manganese oxide—for example, clay-with-flints. In the former case the oxidation of the pyrites produces sulphuric acid, which modifies some soil minerals, and in the latter case the manganese oxides catalyse the reaction, causing the violent emission of oxygen (Catt and Weir, 1975).

(1) Place the sample in a large beaker (1–2 litre) and slowly add sufficient 15% H_2O_2 to cover. Stir gently with a glass rod, taking care not to crush the grains.

(2) After a short time the mixture will start to 'boil', giving off water vapour and oxygen as a white smoke. If this reaction has not started within 10 min, a little heat may be applied *very gently*, and a few millilitres of potassium hydroxide (KOH) added. Allow the mixture to stand.

(3) When the reaction has stopped, usually after several hours, pour off the peroxide and wash the sample several times with distilled water. If the greater part of the organic material has not been removed, the process should be repeated.

(4) Dry the sample as described above (p. 38).

Care must be taken to avoid getting H_2O_2 on skin or clothes.

REMOVAL OF CARBONATES

The following method is the most suitable, but is not recommended if a mineralogical analysis is contemplated (Ingram, 1971):

(1) Place the sample in a large beaker (250–500 cm³). Add 25 ml deionised water and stir gently.
(2) Add 10% HCl until the effervescence stops. If the reaction is slow, heat *gently* to about 80–90 °C until the reaction is complete.

Alternatively, 10% HCl may be added until the pH of the sample is equal to 5.4, measured on a pH meter (p. 67). A high percentage of carbonate hinders the removal of organic matter with hydrogen peroxide, and precipitates calcium oxide if the suggested method for the removal of iron oxides is tried. After removal of carbonates the residue should be washed and dried, and the weight loss recorded.

Decalcification may also be carried out with acetic acid buffered at pH 5, which is preferable to the HCl method, since the latter also dissolves the phosphates present in the sample. The resulting acetates should be removed by washing and centrifuging (Catt and Weir, 1975).

REMOVAL OF IRON OXIDES

This procedure is a necessary preliminary to the examination of highly ferruginous sands or gravels, especially if grain surface textures are to be described.

(1) Place sample in a 500 cm³ beaker. Add distilled water to cover until the total content of the beaker is about 300 cm³.
(2) Put some aluminium into the mixture (a small sheet of cylinder aluminium is suitable).
(3) Add 15 g of concentrated solution of oxalic acid and boil *gently* for 10–20 min. Add more acid if required to raise the concentration (Leith, 1950). Iron oxides may also be removed with dithionite citrate (Mehra and Jackson, 1960), or ammonium oxalate under ultra-violet irradiation (Le Riche and Weir, 1963).

References

BREWER, R. and BARROW, K. J. (1972). 'A microsplitter for subsampling small particulate samples', *Journal of Sedimentary Petrology*, **42** (2), 485–487

CATT, J. A. and WEIR, A. H. (1975). 'The study of archaeologically important sediments by petrographic techniques', in *Geoarchaeology: Earth Science and the Past*, ed. Davidson, D. A. and Shackley, M. L. (Duckworth, London)

GENRICH, D. A. and BREMNER, J. M. (1972). 'A re-evaluation of the ultrasonic vibration method of dispersing soils', *Proceedings of the Soil Science Society of America*, **36** (6), 944–947

INGRAM, R. L. (1971). 'Sieve analysis', in *Procedures in Sedimentary Petrology*, ed. Carver, R. (Wiley, New York)

LEITH, C. J. (1950). 'Removal of iron oxide coatings from mineral grains', *Journal of Sedimentary Petrology*, **20**, 174–179

LE RICHE, H. H. and WEIR, A. H. (1963). 'A method of studying trace elements in soil fractions', *Journal of Soil Science*, **14**, 225–235

MEHRA, O. P. and JACKSON, M. L. (1960). 'Iron oxide removal from soils and clays by a dithionite –citrate system buffered with sodium bicarbonate', *Clays and Clay Mineralogy*, **7**, 311–327

Chapter 5

DESCRIBING GRAIN CHARACTERISTICS

MEASUREMENT OF GRAIN SIZE

DIRECT MEASUREMENT

The component grains of a coarse sediment, especially boulders and cobbles larger than 100 mm in diameter, must be sized by some direct method, since it is impractical to transport a sufficiently large sample back to the laboratory. Doehring and Clausen (1967) in advocating direct field measurement for large particles note that alternative methods produce errors and make the definition of depositional environments extremely difficult.

The technique of pebble measurement has been described by Pettijohn (1949), and involves measuring the dimensions of the three main axes of the particle, namely the long (a) axis, the short (c) axis and the intermediate (b) axis (*Figure 5.1*). This may be done very simply in either the field or the laboratory by the use of a graduated tape, rule and graph paper, or preferably by the use of calipers. If a large sample is to be measured, the construction of a simple apparatus such as that shown in *Figure 5.1* is advisable. This consists of a flat piece of wood, covered with metric graph paper, with two narrow pieces of wood (graduated in millimetres) nailed to it to form a right angle. The third arm may be left free or constructed so that it slides along one of the others. The pebble to be measured is placed at the junction of the fixed arms and the readings of the a and b axes are taken directly. It is then rotated so that the c axis can be measured, and held in place by the sliding arm. The ingenious method of Burke and Freeth (1969), using an overhead projector, is easier for laboratory measurements. The pebbles are placed on a transparent sheet of graph paper on the projector, and are spread out with their a and b axes parallel to the surface. The measurements can then be read directly, and the length of the c axis is found by rotating the particle until this dimension reaches a minimum value. The method is an improvement on the 'fixed block' described above, since the effect of parallax is eliminated. In all direct size measurements a

42

representative sample is constituted by at least 300 pebbles. The results should be recorded in simple tabular form.

The measurement of curved surfaces, radii or diameters is more difficult, and a set of curved templates is recommended. The process then involves the placing of a transparent circular scale (Pryor, 1971) over the corner to be measured.

Hardcastle (1971) devised a pebble measurer for laboratory use giving a punched tape output, which greatly speeds up the process. Tester and Bay (1931) used a 'shapeometer' for a similar purpose.

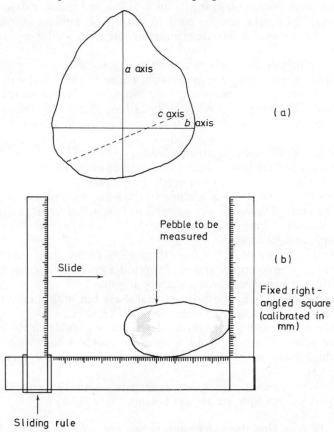

Fig. 5.1. (a) The three axes of a particle; (b) A simple apparatus for measuring the dimensions of large particles

Griffiths (1967) recommends that the measured results of such analyses be transferred from the metric to the logarithmic ϕ scale (p. 91), for ease in later mathematical treatment. It is usual to express results as axial ratios (e.g. a/b, c/b), rather than to leave them as simple measurements, and these ratios can then be plotted as graphs or histograms for inter-sample comparison (p. 94). Excellent results may often be obtained by comparing different populations using simple statistical tests such as Student's t or χ^2. The writer has found that it is possible to characterise and distinguish pebble populations in gravel and cobble deposits by these means, and in some measure to define depositional environments.

GRAIN SHAPE

The roundness and flatness of particle shape are significant indicators of depositional environment, stratigraphic horizons and certain palaeoclimatic conditions. They may also be used to distinguish pebbles belonging to different populations, and to determine the rate of downslope movements of sediments.

There are numerous methods for describing the shape of a grain, some which involve comparing the grain with standard charts, and some which rely on accurate measurements, or combinations of these measurements into indices. The simplest method of describing shape is by reference to a verbal scale, an example of which is summarised below (*Figure 5.2*).

Shape of Grains or Grain Aggregates ('Peds')
  (1) *Platy.* Platelike grains with a vertical axis much less prominent than the other two. Grain faces nearly horizontal.
  (2) *Prismatic.* The grain is arranged prism-like around a vertical face. The vertical faces are well defined and the actual vertices angular.
  (3) *Columnar.* A grain shape similar to the prismatic, except that the grain caps are well rounded.
  (4) *Angular blocky.* Here the three dimensions of the grain are of similar orders of magnitude, arranged around a point. The grain faces are flattened and most vertices sharply angular.
  (5) *Subangular blocky.* A similar general shape but with mixed rounded and flattened faces with many rounded vertices.
  (6) *Granular.* A sediment may be described as granular if the particles are relatively non-porous spheres or polyhedrons, with surfaces which have no accommodation to the faces of the surrounding grains.
  (7) *Crumbs.* Crumbs are grain aggregates with the same shape as granules, but they are always porous.

It can be seen that these descriptions are not only qualitative but also extremely subjective. Different operators have quite a different view of the shapes described, and it is difficult to attain any degree of standardisation in grain descriptions done by this means. However, the classification is simple and quick, but the use of quantitative shape parameters is always to be preferred, except for very perfunctory field description.

The triangular-shape diagram of Sneed and Folk (1958) is a useful way of describing pebble shape by reference to axial ratio measurements (p. 46). This is time-saving, since the values used will usually have already been calculated if a direct size analysis (p. 42) has been undertaken. The method

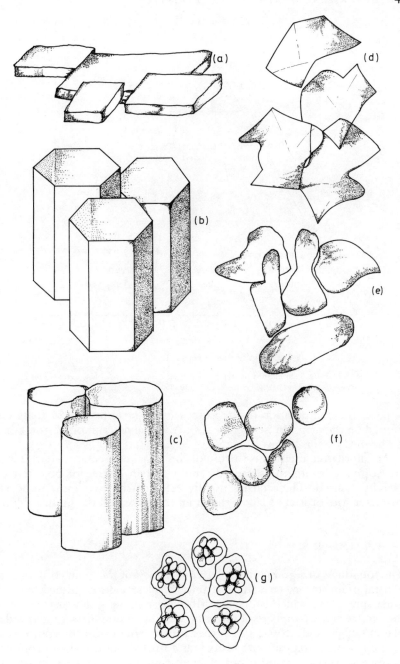

*Fig. 5.2. Shape descriptions of particles: (a) platy; (b) prismatic; (c) columnar; (d) angular blocky;
(e) subangular blocky; (f) granular; (g) crumbs*

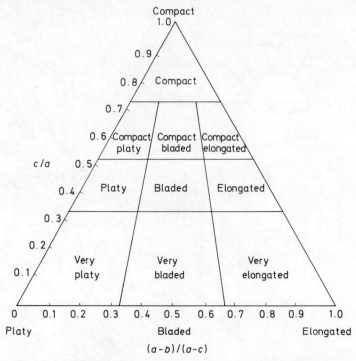

Fig. 5.3. A triangular diagram for expressing the shape of pebbles: (a) long axis; (b) inter-mediate axis; (c) short axis (after Sneed and Folk, 1958)

requires the computation of the ratios c/a and $(a–b)/(a–c)$, which are then plotted on the diagram (see *Figure 5.3*). A verbal description of grain shape is obtained by this means.

An alternative method is the use of the visual comparator chart. Grains are compared with the standards and a certain degree of objectivity is thereby assured. These charts usually refer to the two most important characteristics of grain shape—the grain *roundness* and the grain *sphericity*.

ROUNDNESS

The roundness of a grain is the relative sharpness of the grain corners or the general grain surface curvature. It must be clearly distinguished from the grain sphericity, which is best described by relating grain surface area to the surface area of a sphere of the same volume. Roundness is independent of grain shape, and is to a large degree a function of the mineral composition of the grain, its depositional history and final depositional environment. Numerous verbal classifications of grain roundness have been made—for example, those of Russell and Taylor (1937) and Pettijohn (1949). Many methods have also been devised for the mathematical expression of roundness indices, the most widely used being those of Wadell (1933)

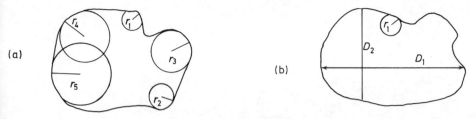

(a)

(b)

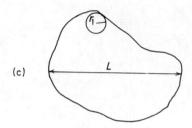

(c)

Fig. 5.4. Calculation of roundness indices: (a) after Wadell (1933); (b) after Wentworth (1933); (c) after Cailleux (1947)

(*Figure 5.4a*), Wentworth (1933) (*Figure 5.4b*) and Cailleux (1942) (*Figure 5.4c*), all of whom constructed roundness indices based on various parameters measured from the grains.

Wadell's roundness index (P_d)

$$P_d = \frac{\Sigma \left(\frac{r}{R}\right)}{n} \tag{5.1}$$

where r = curvature radius of individual corners; n = number of corner radii, including corners whose radii are zero; and R = radius of maximum inscribed circle.

Wentworth's roundness ratio (P_r)

$$P_r = \frac{r_1}{R} \tag{5.2}$$

where r_1 = radius of smallest corner; $R = (D_1+D_2)/4$ = mean grain radius; D_1 = longest dimension of grain; and D_2 = greatest width of grain, normal to D_1.

Cailleux rounding index (P_i)

$$P_i = \frac{2r_1}{L} \tag{5.3}$$

where r_1 = radius of smallest corner, and L = greatest length.

Powers (1958) combined the Wadell calculation (P_d) with descriptive roundness classes, as did Pettijohn (1949) and Folk (1955). The Powers

48

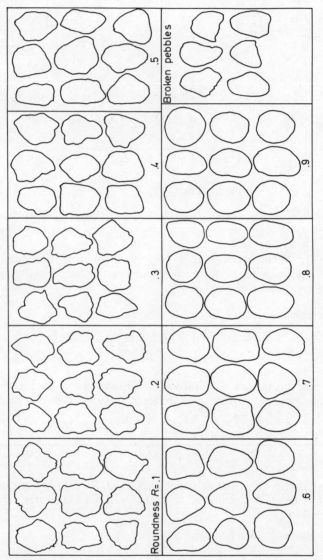

Fig. 5.5. Images for estimating visual roundness (after Powers, 1958)

visual comparator chart (*Figure 5.5*) is the most widely used device for grain roundness description, although Griffiths (1967) has pointed out various difficulties inherent in its use. It is particularly useful for quick shape description, but if the grain shape is likely to be a particularly significant factor, then one of the indices described above should be calculated from measured parameters. These can be taken either from a hand specimen or from a thin section or grain projection.

SPHERICITY

Similar methods have been used for the quantification of particle sphericity, a concept that was first introduced by Wadell (1932). The most commonly used calculated indices are those of Wadell (1935) and Krumbein (1941).

Wadell's working sphericity (ψ_w)

$$\psi_w = \sqrt{\frac{4A_p}{\dfrac{II}{d_p}}}$$

where A_p = projected area of grain, and d_p = diameter of smallest circumscribed circle around grain projection.

Krumbein's intercept sphericity (ψ_1)

$$\psi_1 = \sqrt[3]{\left(\frac{L \times I \times S}{L^2}\right)}$$

where L = longest axis; I = intermediate axis; and S = short axis.

The visual comparator of Rittenhouse (1943) is the most useful method of describing sphericity for archaeological purposes, where great mathematical sophistication is seldom required.

Thomas and Howard (1972) have recently developed a computer program, PEBPROBS, which generates shape and roundness indices for pebbles, and which has now been slightly modified by Crofts (1973, personal communication). The program requires an input composed of the axial measurements of the pebble (p. 43) and will output the raw data, maximum projected area of the pebbles and maximum projected sphericity. It also yields the statistics of the sample distribution.

This type of approach is time-saving and accurate, and permits of the clear presentation of standardised results. The writer has used the program in a study of pebble populations in Pleistocene gravel deposits, and found that it has many applications in distinguishing different groupings and environments of deposition.

A combination of the Powers roundness and Rittenhouse sphericity charts (*Figures 5.5, 5.6*) adequately describes grain shape, although it is worth remembering that any such visual method has a certain operator

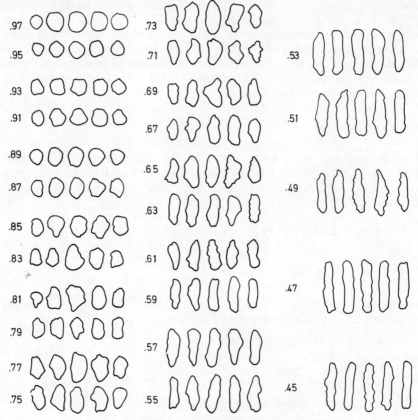

Fig. 5.6. Images for estimating visual sphericity (after Rittenhouse, 1943)

error (Griffiths, 1967). Results may be obtained in tabular form, and then expressed by means of a graph or histogram. Different populations of pebbles may be distinguished in this way.

Figure 5.7 shows a histogram of the visual roundness and sphericity measurements obtained from the analysis of a gravel stratum at Great Pan Farm, Newport, Isle of Wight, which had proved particularly rich in fresh Mousterian artifacts. The composition of the deposit was described by a detailed particle size analysis, combined with work on the particle orientation and grain characteristics. The gravel was composed of a mixed population of heavily abraded chert pebbles and fresh flint gravel, and was thought to have been partly derived from erosion of local beds of Greensand (for the chert) and Chalk (for the flint). It can be seen from the histogram that the roundness values of the chert and flint pebbles differed significantly, although the sphericity values were similar. It has long been realised that roundness is intimately related to the degree of transport that the particle has undergone, and that the most highly rounded particles have often been undergoing transport for extremely long periods of time.

The initial rounding is quite rapid, but then slows down. In this case the high degree of rounding evident in the chert pebbles suggests that they might well have been redeposited, and it is thought that this fraction of the gravel originated in re-worked ancient high-level terrace gravels, although the extremely low degree of rounding of the flint particles suggests that

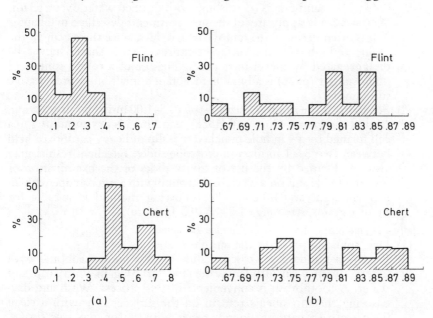

Fig. 5.7. Roundness (a) and sphericity (b) measurements for flint and chert pebbles from gravels at Newport, Isle of Wight

this re-worked gravel was combined with freshly eroded material. The hardness of the two materials is not significantly different, and the roundness values are thought to represent a true difference in the amount of erosion rather than a reflection of the different materials. The history of the deposit is clarified by this simple test, which must be supplemented by a particle size analysis.

GRAIN SURFACE TEXTURES

The surface textures of quartz sand grains usually show characteristics that help in determining their origin and depositional history, and as such provide a valuable source of information. Surface textures may be described either by examining the grains under a low-power light microscope or by the use of more sophisticated methods involving a scanning electron microscope. A combination of surface texture description and particle size analysis should enable the origin of a sediment to be determined with some accuracy.

LIGHT MICROSCOPY

SAMPLE PREPARATION AND MOUNTING

Method A
  (1) Prepare the sand grains by washing with distilled water over a 63 μm (4 ϕ) sieve, and apply any of the pre-treatments described in Chapter 3. It is often necessary to remove iron oxides, since these cement the grains and obscure the surface textures. Grains should never be disaggregated by use of ultrasonics. The use of a rotary splitter or microsplitter (p. 36) is advisable to obtain a small but representative sub-sample.
  (2) Separate off the grains of sizes 1–0 ϕ (0.5–1.00 mm), by dry sieving.
  (3) Mount the grains. Cornwall (1958) recommends dry mounting in a cell formed by a $\frac{3}{4}$ in hole punched in a slip of heavy cardboard held between two 3×1 in glass microscope slides. Excellent results may also be obtained by the use of cavity slides or the examination of unmounted grains on a black background with a microscope with an incident light attachment. The following method is suitable for smaller grains, size range 1.5–1ϕ (0.3–0.5 mm).

Method B (mounting fine sand in Canada Balsam)
  (1) Dry, split and pre-treat the sample as above.
  (2) Prepare a standard microscope slide by thorough scrubbing with xylene, wash with distilled water and scrub again with soap and water. A toothbrush is convenient for this process. Wash and dry, ensuring that no smears remain on the surface. Dry with a clean linen cloth or natural sponge; never with cotton wool or tissues, since these leave fragments.
  (3) Heat a small hot plate to 80 °C, and cover with medium-weight paper to prevent staining due to spilt chemicals.
  (4) Put the slide on the hot plate, and cover half of it with a thick coat of Canada Balsam. Leave for 15 min at 80 °C. Sprinkle evenly at least 100 fine sand grains on to the hot Balsam, and leave for another 5 min. Resist the temptation to modify the distribution of the grains with any small instruments, since this causes air bubbles.
  (5) Clean a coverslip as in stage (2) above, using great care since coverslips are very fragile. Position this over the grains without disturbing them.
  (6) Remove the slide from the hot plate and cool in air for a few moments. If the slide was heated for the correct time, the Canada Balsam will have set and will hold the grains firmly. Excess Balsam may be removed from around the coverslip with a soft cloth soaked in xylene.
  (7) Clean the slide.

This method ensures a permanent mount and does not affect or obscure the surface textures. A little practice is needed to obtain exactly the right quantity of Canada Balsam, since too little will not hold the grains and too much will spread all over the hot plate. If the recommended grain size limits are exceeded, then the coverslip will not hold but will 'balance' on the grains. If air bubbles appear after the coverslip has been put on, then the slide should be left longer on the hot plate. If the bubbles persist, tap the coverslip *very gently* with the edge of a spatula to spread the Balsam. Energetic tapping results in a cracked coverslip and more bubbles. Bubbles will form around the grains if the Balsam was initially heated for too short a time, but may be removed after dropping the coverslip on by 'painting' more Balsam around its edges. This, however, results in a messy slide that will need thorough cleaning. On no account should the xylene be allowed to come in contact with the fingers, since it is carcinogenic. The entire preparation should ideally be done in a fume cupboard to avoid inhaling xylene; but if this is not possible, position the hot plate under an extractor fan and avoid breathing in the fumes.

EXAMINATION OF THE GRAINS

Cailleux (1942) distinguished four principal varieties of sand grains:

(1) *Unworn angular grains.* These are of recent origin, having been freshly produced by some form of weathering, and have angular edges and low roundness values (p. 48). They appear 'clean' under the microscope and often rather shiny.

(2) *Worn, rounded, and glossy grains.* Cailleux considered that this type of surface texture indicated the action of running water, and the characteristics are found on sand grains from marine or fluviatile deposits. Roundness values of this type of grain tend to be rather high.

(3) *Clean, well-rounded matt-surfaced grains.* The surface of the grain has been dulled by wind action. The grains may occasionally be faceted but usually have high roundness and sphericity values.

(4) *'Dirty', rounded and matt-surfaced grains.* This texture is quite unmistakable. The grains are coated with many tiny particles that give them a 'dusty' appearance under the microscope. The effect is produced by a coating of small grains of the original cement, since the grains are likely to have been recently derived from the weathering of older sandstones or similar rocks.

In practice these distinctions are easy to make, and the student can assemble a 'reference' collection of sand grains derived from known environments. Such a simple description of grain type is an aid to sediment characterisation, and the method may be semi-quantified by counting the number of grains of each type present and expressing the results as percentages of the whole. Care must be taken to count sufficient grains for statistical accuracy (Cailleux, 1945, 1947). The distinctions between the classes are obviously much too vague and subjective, and since much of the early work was concerned principally with the recognition of aeolian action within the Pleistocene deposits of Europe, wider applications should be considered with great caution. The method is useful for distinguishing freshly weathered sand grains, and those immediately derived from local outcrops in sediments with mixed populations, but it is too unrefined for more accurate observations.

SCANNING ELECTRON MICROSCOPY

The scanning electron microscope (or SEM) offers a more sophisticated and accurate way of describing surface textures, although the method still relies on the hypothesis that the surface texture accurately reflects the depositional history of the grain. The numerous papers written concerning the method have recently been summarised by Krinsley and Doornkamp (1973). These writers consider that it is possible to distinguish certain depositional environments from surface textures, but emphasise that various conditions must be borne in mind if quantitative interpretation is planned.

Their definitive variables are described within the broad framework of quartz crystallography, the importance of such features as flat cleavage plates, conchoidal breakage patterns and the surface precipitation of silica

Table 5.1   DIAGENETIC SURFACE CHARACTERISTICS OF QUARTZ SAND GRAINS
(AFTER KRINSLEY AND DOORNKAMP, 1973)

Marine, fluviatile and lacustrine environments

High-energy (surf)	Medium- and low-energy
(1) V-shaped patterns of irregular orientation	(1) 'En echelon' V-shaped indentations at low energy. As energy increases, random orientated V-patterns replace them
(2) Straight or slightly curved grooves	
(3) Blocky conchoidal breakage patterns	

Aeolian

Tropical desert	Coastal dune
(1) Meandering ridges	(1) Meandering ridges
(2) Graded arcs	(2) Graded arcs
(3) Chemical or mechanical action giving regular pitted surfaces replacing the above features in many cases	(3) Disc-shaped depressions
(4) Upturned cleavage plates and well-rounded grains	

Glacial

Normal	Glacio-fluvial
(1) Large variations in size of conchoidal breakage patterns	(1) Rounding of the normal glacial patterns
(2) Very high relief	
(3) Semi-paralleled and arc-shaped steps. Parallel striations of varying length	
(4) Imbricated breakage blocks which look like a series of steeply dipping hogback ridges	
(5) Irregular small-scale indentations associated with conchoidal breakage patterns	
(6) Prismatic patterns	

especially being recognised. Grain size is considered to be critical, since with grains larger than 2 ϕ (200 μm) conchoidal breakage patterns tend to occur which produce irregular blocks and mask other surface characteristics. It is possible to make useful observations about sediment source, and diagenesis, distinguishing the products of glacial, littoral, aeolian and various other environments. A full discussion of these points may be seen in Krinsley and Doornkamp (1973).

Table 5.1 summarises the important diagenetic surface characteristics of sand grains. Despite a recent paper by Brown (1973) which cast some doubts on the validity of interpretations made by this method, the basic hypothesis seems to be accepted by most workers, if the correct sampling procedures are undertaken.

SAMPLE PREPARATION FOR THE SCANNING ELECTRON MICROSCOPE

(1) Examine the sample under low-power binocular microscope and describe its characteristics.
(2) Place 5 mg of randomly split sample in a beaker, add concentrated HCl and boil gently for about 10 min. Wash thoroughly. It may be necessary to remove iron oxides or organic matter. Wash with distilled water and dry gently.
(3) Select 20 grains at random from the sample, less than 200 μm in diameter (2 ϕ). The metal specimen stub supplied by the manufacturers of the SEM can either be coated with sticky tape to hold the grains or they can be cemented on with silver paint or glue. The plug is then coated with a thin layer of a heavy metal or carbon in a vacuum evaporator. Gold seems to give the best results with sand grains (Bradley, 1965). The stub is then ready to insert into the apparatus. It is usually convenient to prepare several samples together, and in this case a reference number must be gently scratched on the reverse side of the specimen stub.

THE SCANNING ELECTRON MICROSCOPE

The scanning electron microscope is a relatively new instrument, the first having been made by Cambridge Scientific Instruments in 1965 (Oatley, 1958). *Figure 5.8* shows their latest model, the S4-10, and *Figure 5.9* an explanation of the working parts. The specimen stub is placed in a chamber within the vacuum column and is then bombarded with a fine beam of electrons from a tungsten filament. The electron beam is scanned by a detection field and the secondary (emissive) electrons are picked up by a collator to give an image. The small electron probe size and great depth of field means that a specimen can be 'viewed' in three dimensions with great clarity at magnifications from $\times 10$ to $\times 200\,000$. The magnifications are controlled by varying the amount of deflection of the electron beam. The image appears on a double cathode ray tube display, one screen of which is used for viewing and the other for photography. The image may be photographed with a 'Polaroid' camera or a specially fitted camera taking standard 35 mm black and white film. The latter method is preferable since it is often useful to have a negative. The instrument gives very high resolution (about 100 Å), enabling very detailed observations to be made. It is also extremely expensive, at least £20 000, but may be available on a

Fig. 5.8. The Cambridge 'Stereoscan' scanning electron microscope, Model S4-10: (a) vacuum column; (b) specimen chamber; (c) visual raster; (d) record raster with camera. (Reproduced by courtesy of Cambridge Scientific Instruments Ltd)

contract basis from commercial firms or University departments. It is also useful for particle size analysis of very fine materials in the sub-sieve range, and this may be combined with textural description.

Since machine preparation (vacuum cooling, pumping the vacuum down, warming up) is time-consuming, it is always better to process a batch of samples together, since the time required for specimen change is only a few minutes. However, the scan rate on the screen is very tiring on the eyes and the writer has found it impossible to concentrate for more than 1–2 h at a stretch. This figure improves a little with practice. The examination and counting of a single sample will take about half an hour, and once the operating principle of the machine has been grasped the procedure is fairly simple. A few sessions of expert tuition are recommended.

The study of grain surface textures with the SEM has an interesting application in the examination of pottery fabrics. The so-called small 'Carrot'-shaped amphorae (Camulodunum form 189) which were imported into Britain during the first century AD and which are found at numerous important sites—for example, Pompeii, Colchester (Camulodunum), British and German forts—present an interesting problem, since it has hitherto been impossible to diagnose their provenance. Neither a study of the fabrics in thin-section nor an examination of their heavy mineral species proved helpful. It was decided to try a study of the surface textures of quartz particles included in the potting clay, since this might give a clue to the depositional environment of sediments found near the manufacturing site.

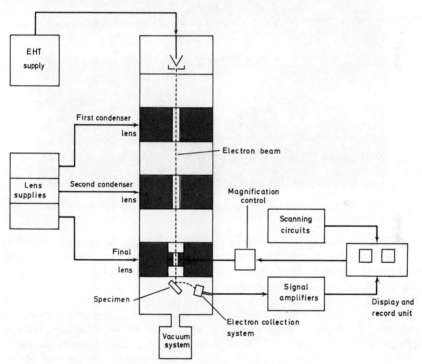

Fig. 5.9. Operating principles of the scanning electron microscope. (Reproduced by courtesy of Cambridge Scientific Instruments Ltd)

A few grams of the fabric of one of the amphora were crushed in a pestle and mortar, and examined under a low-power binocular microscope. The quartz sand grains could be extracted from the crushed clay by a fine brush dipped in water. These were then dried, mounted and examined in the SEM as described above. The grains showed many of the characteristics considered by Krinsley and Doornkamp (1973) to be diagnostic of an aeolian depositional environment, and none of those typical of a littoral or glacial environment. *Figure 5.10* shows a typical rounded

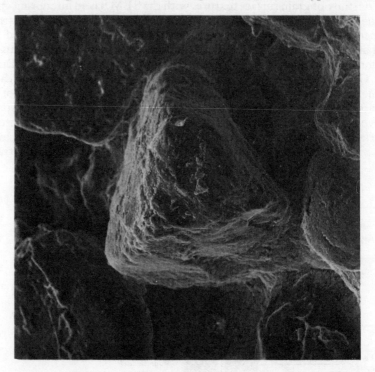

Fig. 5.10. *Scanning electron microscope photograph of a quartz sand grain from a 'Carrot' amphora (magnification × 75)*

grain, selected at random from the population present on the stub, showing a surface texture composed of upturned quartz plates affected by solution and precipitation of silica. This type of grain topography is explained by the action of water evaporating in a desert environment, the 'desert dew' hypothesis. Under hot aeolian conditions each grain tends to pass through a cycle of solution and precipitation when the grains are stationary, followed by erosion when the grain is saltated by wind action. All the grains obtained from the 'Carrot' amphora show these features. It seems likely, therefore, that the provenance of these quartz grains, and of the potting clay, is to be sought in a hot sandy climate, since the aeolian features listed above do not include the gently graded arcs of disc-shaped depressions found on grains from coastal dunes.

It must, however, be remembered that an analysis of this kind has only examined a small area of the fabric of a pot, although it is to be hoped that the sampling procedure was sufficiently random to ensure the accuracy of the results. By way of a control experiment a sherd of known provenance was processed, taken from amphorae produced in the fifth century BC at

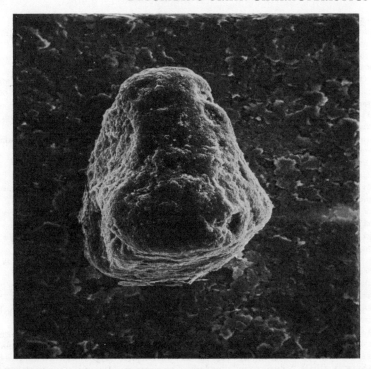

Fig. 5.11. Scanning electron microscope photograph of a quartz sand grain from a Tell Farras amphora (magnification × 75)

the Palestinian site of Tell Faras. *Figure 5.11* shows the surface appearance of one of these grains, which is virtually identical with those from the 'Carrot' amphorae. Since the hot desert environment of the Tell Faras pottery is well documented, this evidence lends support to the theory that the origin of the 'Carrot' amphorae is to be sought in a region of similar climatic conditions. This field would appear to hold great potential for applied sedimentology.

References

BRADLEY, D. E. (1965). 'Replica and shadowing techniques', in *Techniques for Electron Microscopy*, ed. Kay, D. (Blackwell, London)

BROWN, J. E. (1973). 'Depositional histories of sand grains from surface textures', *Nature (Lond.)*, **242**, 396–398

BURKE, K. and FREETH, S. J. (1969). 'A rapid method for the determination of shape, sphericity and size of gravel particles', *Journal of Sedimentary Petrology*, **39** (2), 797–798

CAILLEUX, A. (1942). 'Les actions éoliennes périglaciares en Europe', *Memoire de la Société Géologique de France*, **21** (146)

CAILLEUX, A. (1945). 'Distinction des galets marins et fluviatiles', *Bull. Soc. Géologique de France*, **25**, 375–404

CAILLEUX, A. (1947). 'Granulométrie des formations à galets', in *La géologie des terrains récent dans l'ouest de l'Europe*, 91–114 (Rep. Extraord. Sessions Soc. Belges Géol.)

CORNWALL, I. W. (1958). *Soils for the Archaeologist* (Phoenix, London)

DOEHRING, D. and CLAUSEN, E. N. (1967). 'The analysis of coarse clastic grains using standard statistical methods', *Wyoming University Contributions in Geology*, **6** (2), 87–92

FOLK, R. L. (1955). 'Student operator error in determination of roundness, sphericity and grain size', *Journal of Sedimentary Petrology*, **25**, 297–301

GRIFFITHS, J. C. (1967). *Scientific Method in the Analysis of Sediments* (McGraw-Hill, New York)

HARDCASTLE, P. J. (1971). 'A pebble measurer for laboratory use giving a punched tape output', *Journal of Sedimentary Petrology*, **41** (4), 1138–1140

KRINSLEY, D. H. and DOORNKAMP, J. C. (1973). *Atlas of Quartz Grain Surface Textures* (Cambridge University Press)

KRUMBEIN, W. C. (1941). 'Measurement and geologic significance of shape and roundness of sedimentary particles', *Journal of Sedimentary Petrology*, **11**, 64–72

OATLEY, C. W. (1958). 'The scanning electron microscope', *New Scientist*, **5**, 153–178

PETTIJOHN, F. J. (1949). *Sedimentary Rocks* (Harper and Row, New York)

POWERS, M. C. (1958). 'Roundness of sedimentary particles. Comparison chart for visual estimation of roundness', *A.G.I. Data Sheet for Geotimes*, **3** (1), 15–16

PRYOR, W. A. (1971). 'Grain shape', in *Procedures in Sedimentary Petrology*, ed. Carver, R. (Wiley, New York)

RUSSELL, P. D. and TAYLOR, R. E. (1937). 'Roundness and shape of Mississippi river sands', *Journal of Geology*, **45**, 225–267

RITTENHOUSE, G. (1943). 'A visual method of estimating two-dimensional sphericity', *Journal of Sedimentary Petrology*, **13**, 79–81

SNEED, E. D. and FOLK, R. L. (1958). 'Pebbles in the lower Colorado river, Texas: a study in particle morphogenesis', *Journal of Geology*, **66**, 114–150

TESTER, A. C. and BAY, H. X. (1931). 'The shapeometer: a device for measuring the shape of pebbles', *Science*, **73**, 565–566

THOMAS, J. B. and HOWARD, B. A. (1972). 'PEBPROBS—a Fortran IV programme for calculation of particle size and shape from field data' (private paper used in the London School of Economics)

WADELL, H. A. (1932). 'Volume, shape and roundness of rock particles', *Journal of Geology*, **40**, 443–451

WADELL, H. A. (1933). 'Sphericity and roundness of rock particles', *Journal of Geology*, **41**, 310–331

WADELL, H. A. (1935). 'Volume, shape and roundness of quartz particles', *Journal of Geology*, **43**, 250–280

WENTWORTH, C. K. (1933). 'The shapes of rock particles: a discussion', *Journal of Geology*, **41**, 306–309

Chapter 6

MEASURING CHEMICAL CHARACTERISTICS

ANALYTICAL TECHNIQUES

The measurement of the chemical composition of a sediment often involves the use of highly sophisticated techniques and instruments. Chemical analysis at a quantitative level requires specialised knowledge, and the reader is referred to the standard works on soil chemistry by Jackson (1962) and Hesse (1971) for a study of the theoretical basis of the methods and a fuller description of experimental procedures. The aspects of soil and sediment chemistry that have generally been considered important for archaeological purposes include quantitative determination of carbon, humus, phosphates and iron, and the identification of other materials present in the sediment in small quantities. Wet chemical and colorimetric techniques are often used, supplemented by X-ray diffraction analysis for clay mineral composition, or atomic absorption analysis for trace elements. Some of the problems presented by the chemical analysis of archaeological sediments are discussed by Catt and Weir (1975), and many of the relevant laboratory techniques by Cornwall (1958). Little chemical work can be undertaken in the field, only the measurement of pH and phosphate presence being really practical, but several papers are available (for example, Cornwall, 1959; Lutz, 1951; Mattingly and Wilson, 1962) in which the results of field sediment description are combined with chemical tests completed later in the laboratory. Mulvaney and Joyce (1965) determined variations in the phosphorus content of a series of sediments from the Kenniff cave (Queensland, Australia), using a spectrophotometer, and combined the results (expressed in ppm of elemental phosphorus) with determinations of the total carbonate content. These chemical properties and a note of changes in particle size composition illustrated the main occupation phases of the cave. A similarly structured approach was used by Biek (1960) and Cornwall (1960) in reports on various aspects of buried soils.

COLORIMETRY

Colorimetry is a method for measuring the concentrations of certain compounds present in solutions by measuring the intensity of their colour. This is usually done by comparing the colour of the test solution with a graph or series of standards produced by the analysis of solutions of known concentration. Since colour measurement is normally a subjective judgment, the use of a colorimeter enables it to be expressed numerically. Colorimeters are fast, simple and easy to work, and each is used with a series of filters to remove certain components of the light passing through the solutions.

In the Pye-Unicam SP1300 Series 2 colorimeter (*Figure 6.1*) light from a krypton-filled tungsten lamp is focused by a lens through the selected

Fig. 6.1. The Pye-Unicam colorimeter Model SP1300. (Reproduced by courtesy of Pye-Unicam Ltd)

filter into the 10 mm sample container. The filters are mounted on a rotatable disc and are selected from the Ilford Bright Spectrum range. The sample container requires about 2.8 ml of solution, and light intensity readings are taken from a light spot on a galvanometer scale calibrated in transmittance and absorbance. Results are reproducible to $\pm 0.25\%$[10]. The instrument can be combined with an autocell accessory if large quantities of samples have to be processed. The EEL concentration colorimeter[11] has an optional digital readout facility for results. A direct linear reading in response to sample concentration is obtained, or expressed in optical density units. This means that no calibration graphs are required. This model has nine filters, including an initial nominal density filter which is calibrated against known reference standards. This filter is used when the measurements are made. Colorimetric methods are particularly suitable for the quantitative determination of phosphates and humus, and Shukla and Singh (1968) used them to estimate soil nitrate content.

X-RAY DIFFRACTION

Diffraction analysis reveals the arrangement of the atoms and molecules within crystals; and if a mineral within a sediment is crystalline, then it may be detected by this means. Diffraction analysis has recently become an important new field in soil chemistry, since it permits of the qualitative and quantitative determination of the substances present. The technique involves mounting the specimen, bombarding it with a beam of monochromatic X-rays and interpreting the diffraction patterns produced. The structure of the majority of soil minerals has already been worked out, and reference standards are available (p. 79). A crystalline specimen produces a series of X-ray intensities (the diffraction pattern) which are determined by the spacings between the crystal lattice planes of the constituent minerals. The method depends on the Bragg relationship summarised by Tite (1973) and is particularly useful for identifying clay mineral suites. In X-ray powder diffraction the diffraction pattern is produced on to a photographic film as a series of arcs. Mineral identification is made by comparing the distances between pairs of arcs, calculating the associated crystal lattice spacings and comparing these data with the lattice spacings for known minerals. Since the blackening of the arcs depends on the intensity of the reflected X-rays, a semi-quantitative idea of the mineral concentration can be obtained. Methods for mounting and processing specimens by X-ray diffraction are described by Jackson (1962) and Hesse (1971); the sensitivity of the powder diffraction method depends on the mineral concerned and can vary between 1 and 10%.

ATOMIC ABSORPTION SPECTROPHOTOMETER

The atomic absorption spectrophotometer is an accurate way of obtaining a quantification of the presence of small amounts of various substances in a sediment, and has been much used for trace element analysis. Ward *et al.* (1969) provide a general guide to the potential of the instrument in geochemistry, and West (1971) discusses its application to the study of trace metals in soils. The relationship between the survival of trace metals on archaeological sites and time scales has been discussed by Sokoloff and Carter (1952).

Figure 6.2 shows the Pye-Unicam SP90 instrument. The radiation characteristic of the element to be determined is emitted by the appropriate hollow cathode lamp. The radiation beam is focused through a flame (air/acetylene mixture), where it is quantitatively absorbed by the atoms of the element being analysed, and the beam passes through a monochromator on to a photomultiplier detector. The concentration readout may be made directly, and is obtained by measuring the extent to which the light is absorbed. The sample must be submitted in solution, and a different lamp is required for each element. These lamps are mounted in a turret at the end of the instrument. The sample (weight 1–10 g) must be dissolved, usually in a mixture of hydrofluoric and perchloric acids, but Tite (1973)

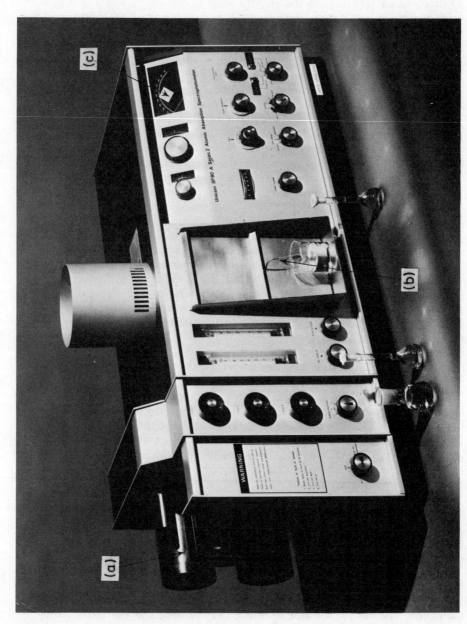

Fig. 6.2. The Pye–Unicam SP90 atomic absorption spectrophotometer: (a) lamp mounting; (b) sample aspiration tube; (c) meter-readout. (Reproduced by courtesy of Pye–Unicam Ltd)

recommends the use of aqua regia as a solvent for metals. A beaker containing the sample is placed under the tube capillary (*Figure 6.2*) and a few millilitres is aspirated into the instrument. The appropriate lamp for the element whose concentration is required must be already in place, and analysis for a series of different elements is done by changing the lamp and aspirating further samples. Accuracy is about ± 1–2%, and the optimum concentration range of the element in solution is 1–10 ppm (1–10 mg/ml). If an element is very abundant, the high concentration necessitates appropriate dilution, with a corresponding decrease of accuracy.

The instrument may be used to detect the presence of phosphates and sulphates, as well as quantitative amounts of the majority of metals and rare earths. The writer has used it successfully to diagnose the contents of soil stains that the excavator thought might represent decayed metal, although the tedious sample preparation involved makes other, less accurate, methods more suitable for this purpose.

Brunelle *et al.* (1969) discuss the use of the atomic absorption spectrophotometer and neutron activation analysis for determining chemical elements in soils. They consider that the former method is preferable, and suggest an initial sample pre-treatment of grinding, crushing and sieving.

Similar techniques have recently been used by Sieveking *et al.* (1972) for the trace element analysis of flint samples, as an aid to the characterisation of the products of various British and West European flint mines. The flint samples were dissolved in a mixture of 40% hydrofluoric acid and 60% perchloric acid, in a Teflon beaker on a water bath. The solutions produced were analysed for calcium, magnesium, aluminium and iron by atomic absorption spectroscopy, and for sodium and potassium by flame emission spectroscopy. Phosphorus content was estimated by the molybdenum blue method of Murphy and Riley (1962), by solution spectroscopy. The ratios between the trace elements formed a consistent pattern for each mine, and statistically valid differences could be recognised between mines. The measured trace element differences were probably due to the clay minerals, and the variations in the composition of the flint were expressed in terms of its mode of origin in the chalk.

CHEMICAL ANALYSIS

pH MEASUREMENTS

The pH (hydrogen ion concentration) is a measure of the relative acidity or alkalinity of the sediment, a property which to a large extent governs the type of chemical processes that can take place within it. Pure water (chemically neutral) contains 10^{-7} of H^+ ions per litre, and therefore has a pH value of 7. More hydrogen ions increase the acidity, so that a pH value lower than 7 denotes acidity, and a value higher than 7 the presence of an alkali. The majority of sediments have values between 5 and 9, although the pH scale ranges from 0 to 14.

Various chemical processes in the sediment determine and influence the pH values, as do the mineral constituents and moisture status. The pH of the soil affects the preservation of organic matter, and an acid soil will help the decomposition of bone and plant material. Calcium phosphate is affected by humic and carbonic acids in the ground and will produce phosphoric acid, which is then leached out. The pH values of sediments developed in calcareous environments—for example, in caves and rock shelters—will usually be high, as on chalk or limestones, but will be low on heathlands, which are acid.

pH MEASUREMENT

There are several methods available to measure sediment pH, the best being the electronic pH meter. Soil pH values vary with the method of preparation, and with factors such as the soil moisture content, the amount of drying done during preparation, the content of soluble salts and the amount of grinding. Jackson (1962) considers that field pH measurement is the most valid. It must always be remembered that the more dilute the sediment suspension the higher the pH value, and some degree of standardisation in preparation is therefore required.

The simplest (and most inaccurate) method of measuring pH is by the use of test papers. These are manufactured in small books[2]. Johnson's 'Universal papers' measure pH in a range from 1 to 11, and are supplied with a colour chart in steps of 1 pH. Colour may be estimated to 0.5 pH, which is not sufficiently accurate. The same firm manufacture 'Comparator' papers, which have a colour chart graduated in steps of 0.3 pH, and accurate determination to within 0.15 pH is possible. Readings are taken by dipping the papers into a sediment suspension, shaking off the excess fluid and comparing the colour with a chart inside the book cover. A better reading is obtained by comparing the colour with a buffer solution of the same value. The presence of proteins will upset the use of indicator papers, as will the inclusion of chloride salts or sulphur dioxide in the sediments.

A slightly more accurate method of measuring pH is to use an indicator. Some substances (such as phenolphthalein) show a marked change of colour at different pH values, and can therefore be used to measure the values. However, this would be a tedious method and the use of indicator solutions such as the BDH 'Universal' indicator is recommended instead. A small amount of the sediment is mixed with distilled water in a test tube and a few drops of the suspension (without any large sediment grains) is transferred to a piece of white glazed tile. One or two drops of the indicator is added and the colour is compared with the standards. Cornwall (1958) recommends the use of the BDH 'Capillator' outfit for site work, but it is inconvenient owing to the necessity of continually rinsing glasses and equipment. A pH meter is the only really reliable way of measuring pH, although in its absence the use of test papers or indicator solutions is preferable to nothing.

The meter measures the 'effective' pH of a sediment, including all sources of hydrogen ions such as those produced by the dissolution of soluble acids. The effective pH is the electrical potential measured with the glass electrode of the meter. In order to use a meter properly, standard buffers are required, one at pH 4.0 (0.05 M potassium biphthalite) and another at pH 9.0. The sediment sample should be prepared without grinding and should not be allowed to remain in suspension longer than necessary. The sample is mixed to a thin paste, so that the surface of the water-saturated material can be seen to glisten. *Figure 6.3* shows the Pye-Unicam 293 pH meter, a portable instrument excellent for field measurements that will take accurate readings from pH 0 to pH 14. The meter is

Fig. 6.3. The Pye-Unicam Model 293 pH meter. (Reproduced by courtesy of Pye-Unicam Ltd)

powered by Mallory batteries with a life of more than 2 000 h. It may be packed in its own carrying case, and comes with a combined glass and reference electrode. The reading is taken by immersing the electrode in the sample and noting the scale value. A resistance thermometer may be incorporated into the instrument. The electrode must never be allowed to dry out and must be washed off after use with distilled water. If the system is alkaline, it should be passed through acid solution to remove any persistent calcium carbonate that might have formed. Readings are very quick and simple to take, accuracy is ensured, the instrument is light to carry and the only ancillary equipment required is a couple of beakers and a wash bottle for the distilled water. Laville (1975) discusses the measurement of ΔpH, in potassium chloride, which he believes may often be used to detect certain small fluctuations in cave sediment sequences that are not apparent to any other method.

PHOSPHATE ANALYSIS

Phosphate analysis is particularly useful for showing horizons or areas associated with bone material (for example, occupation or burial sites) where high concentrations have been produced by the decay of human and animal excreta. Schwartz (1967) uses the technique combined with resistivity surveying to locate archaeological sites in southern Switzerland, remarking on the dramatic increase of soil phosphate content near buried tombs. Modern transformations of the landscape—for example, the construction of artificial 'terraces'—tend to have a very low phosphate content (Schwartz, 1967). Applications of phosphate analysis to archaeology have recently been reviewed by Provan (1971) and Proudfoot (1975).

The 'background' phosphate content of some sediments (e.g. sands) is lower than that of others, but many clays and limestone-derived soils contain proportionally more phosphate, derived from mineralised faecal pellets or collophane from fossil remains (Brown and Ollier, 1956). Sandy sediments are often heavily leached, and care must always be taken to avoid samples contaminated by recent additions of phosphates from modern fertilisers. Of all the materials produced by the breakdown of animal matter, phosphates are the most readily 'fixed', and usually survive as the calcium salt.

QUALITATIVE TESTS FOR PHOSPHATES

The standard laboratory test to detect the presence of phosphates is to boil an acid extract of the sediment with ammonium molybdate and nitric acid. A bright canary-yellow precipitate will be produced. The test suggested by Gundlach (1961) and used by Schwartz (1967) is useful in the field, since it can be done in the cold with a minimum of equipment. Here the total phosphate content is being measured, both the organic phosphorus (which is easily absorbed by plants) and the inorganic phosphates present in archaeological deposits (Cook and Heitzer, 1965). Steward and Oades (1972) describe a method for measuring the organic phosphorus alone.

Gundlach field test

(1) Place a small quantity of sediment (50 mg) in the middle of a filter paper held in a Petri dish.

(2) Add 2 drops of a solution composed of ammonium molybdate in sulphuric acid, measured exactly with a dropping pipette.

(3) Leave for a short period ($\frac{1}{2}$–3 min) and then add 2 equal drops of a solution of ascorbic acid.

(4) The liquids are absorbed in the filter paper, and in the presence of phosphates will turn first yellow and then blue. The colour change can be used as a rough guide to the amount of phosphate present, and Schwartz (1967) uses five colour-intensity grades. The amounts of chemicals added (exactly 2 drops of standard concentrations of each solution) are more important than variations in the amount of sediment used. The chemicals are light-sensitive and lose their potency after about 8 weeks.

QUANTITATIVE TESTS FOR PHOSPHATES

Total phosphate content can best be measured quantitatively by colorimetric methods, using the molybdenum-blue reaction. Cornwall (1958) recommends the following method for preparing the sample for the colorimeter:

(1) Boil 1 g of soil with 20 ml 3N H_2SO_4, for 15 min in a water bath, filter, dilute to 100 ml. Add 5 ml of the filtrate to 20 ml of Lorsch's developer (Lorsch, 1940). Return to the water bath, boil for a further 15 min. 10 ml of solution will usually be required for the colorimeter.

(2) Lorsch's developer is a solution composed of 12 g ammonium molybdate, 10 g sodium sulphate and 0.5 g hydroquinone, in 955 ml distilled water and 45 ml concentrated sulphuric acid. The solids are added to the distilled water and the acid added slowly, stirring all the while.

If the EEL colorimeter is used, filter 621 will be required and the colour of the solution must be compared with clear Lorsch reagent. The concentration of the test solution is read from a graph prepared by initially analysing solutions of known phosphate contents, expressed in terms of mg P_2O_5 (Cornwall, 1958). Davidson (1973) determined phosphates colorimetrically by fusing the sediment with sodium carbonate, the results also being expressed as mg g^{-1} P_2O_5 (Muir, 1952).

In a study of the evolution of the tell site at Sitagroi (north-eastern Greece) Davidson combined total phosphate measurements with particle size analysis. An idea of the 'background' phosphate contents of the local soils was obtained by analysing three samples of terra rossa as controls. The results of the phosphate analysis on the tell sediments tended to be rather varied, a feature that had also been noted by Cook and Heitzer (1965). No distinct trend was evident, but the phosphate content seemed to be higher in the upper levels, suggesting either an increase in occupation density in the later phases or increased phosphate content due to more livestock being kept at the site. Another application of phosphate analysis to archaeology can be seen in the work of Rosenfeld (1966), who describes the analysis of a 'red resinous material' associated with burials under a round barrow on Overton Hill, north Wiltshire. She suggests on the basis of carbonate and phosphate measurements that the material represented is collophane (calcium phosphate), produced by the decay of animal material, here probably flesh. The phosphate contents of archaeological soils have been discussed by Dauncey (1952) and Louis (1946). The combination of phosphate analysis with quantitative determination of other compounds is common, particularly with humus and carbonates. Applications are to be found in the works of Cornwall (1960) and Mulvaney and Joyce (1965), discussed below.

CARBON AND CARBONATES

Carbon can be present in a sediment either as organic carbon or as carbon compounds, usually carbonates. Organic carbon may be contributed from charcoal, hearth deposits or burnt bone, and is resistant to the majority of chemical tests. Carbon flecks can often be detected visually by examining the sediment under a stereoscopic microscope, and may be large enough to permit of the identification of the wood present. Methods for measuring the carbon contents of sediments usually measure total carbon, combining organic and inorganic carbon. The organic carbon content of a sediment can be measured by the standard method of Walkely and Black (1934), although this has been criticised by van Moort and de Vries (1970), who claim that it is unreliable owing to the combustion of graphite and pyrite as well. The Walkely–Black method relies on wet combustion of the sample in a dilute H_2SO_4–$K_2Cr_2O_7$ solution, giving an indication of the amount of *easily* oxidised organic carbon. However, it has been shown that the carbon content of soil organic matter varies widely in horizons of the same soil, and the Walkely–Black hypothesis is now not considered to be correct. The method of van Moort and de Vries for measuring organic carbon involves dry combustion after several pre-treatments, and gave very accurate results after previous removal of carbonates.

The total carbon in a sediment can be measured by the Groves wet combustion method (Groves, 1951), where all the carbon is oxidised to carbon dioxide by use of chromic acid and syrupy phosphoric acid, the CO_2 released being collected in absorption tubes. For determining the total carbonate content in a sediment the 'Karbonat-Bombe' of Müller and Gastner (1971) is highly recommended, since it is accurate and easy to use. The instrument measures the pressure of CO_2 produced by treating a sample with HCl in a closed container. This pressure is proportional to the $CaCO_3$ content of the sample. The instrument (*Figure 6.4*) consists of a manometer calibrated in % calcium carbonate, a plastics container inside a glass cylinder and various fittings for closure. The sample of dried and ground material is put into the cylinder, and the plastics container filled with 5 ml of concentrated HCl is lowered in, care being taken to ensure that none spills on the sample. The stoppers and manometer fitting are then screwed down, the whole apparatus shaken and strong effervescence produced. The manometer reading is taken for calcite and aragonite after 10 s. If there is dolomite in the sample, it reacts more slowly and another reading after 10–15 min will be required. After this time, constant pressure is obtained. The volume of gas produced is dependent on the temperature and atmospheric pressure, and the manometer readings must be corrected for these values. The true value of 100% $CaCO_3$ is determined before the beginning of each set of experiments by processing a sample of 1 g of pure $CaCO_3$. The absolute error of the method is $\pm$ 1% CO_2, and the instrument may be obtained from Germany at a cost of about 180 D M[12].

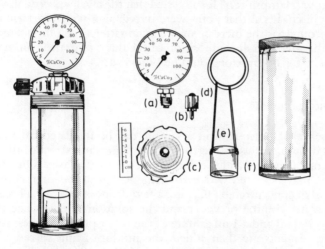

Fig. 6.4. Components of the 'Karbonat-Bombe': (a) manometer; (b) screw and gasket; (c) threaded cap; (d) gasket; (e) plastics container and handle; (f) threaded cylinder (after Müller and Gastner, 1971; see Appendix)

Laville (1975) has discussed the role of carbonate formation and transference in cave environments, applying his methods to some of the most important French cave sequences. Carbonate removal using acid is often important if the particle size composition of a highly calcareous sediment is required, and some quantitative method of measuring it is therefore necessary. The problems presented by carbonate measurements have recently been reviewed by Grant Goss (1971).

ALKALI-SOLUBLE HUMUS

The presence of humus in a sediment can be detected by the production of a brown precipitate after boiling with sodium hydroxide. This principle is also used for the quantitative estimate of humus, usually completed with a colorimeter. The alkali-soluble fraction of soil organic matter is being taken as representative of the whole. A small quantity (1 g) of the sediment is boiled for 1 or 2 min with about 20 ml 3N NaOH, the liquid being filtered off and processed in a colorimeter using a blue filter. Standards need to be made up using 1–10 mg samples of alkali–extracted peat humus, the method being detailed by Cornwall (1958).

The organic matter content of a sediment changes from one type to another, being particularly high in a sediment which was associated with vegetation and particularly low in calcareous environments such as those inside caves. The recognition of changes in organic matter content has often been taken as a means of identifying buried soils and surfaces. Cornwall (1959) used variations in humus and phosphate contents to show up an immature buried turf line in a sequence of ditch silts at the Nutbane long barrow (Hampshire). He suggested that the level was probably formed when the ditch silts at that point were overgrown with vegetation, which would account for the increase in organic matter. The phosphate increase was possibly due to a decomposition of the dung of grazing animals, since no evidence for occupation could be observed.

FERRIC IRON

The presence of ferric iron in a sample can be indicated by a spot test, adding a drop of potassium ferrocyanide to an acid extract of the deposit. The strong 'Prussian Blue' colour indicates ferric iron. Quantitatively ferric iron may be tested with a colorimeter. 1 g of the sediment is heated with 10 ml of concentrated HCl, and a few drops of HNO_3. This is diluted with an equal volume of water and the solution filtered. The filtrate is diluted to 100 ml and a 1 ml sample of the result placed in a test tube. The following reagents are then added, the mixture being stirred after each addition: 0.5 ml citric acid (20% w/v), 1 drop thioglycollic acid, 1 ml ammonia (1 : 3.3 w/v) and water to make a final volume of 10 ml. The violet colour produced is measured in a colorimeter with the appropriate filter, number 626 on the EEL Colorimeter (Cornwall, 1958).

QUANTIFICATION OF THE PRESENCE OF OTHER SUBSTANCES

Quantitative analysis of ferrous iron can be done by the volumetric method of Groves (1951) with potassium permanganate. Quantitative determination of the presence of calcium and magnesium may also be completed volumetrically and that of sodium and potassium by using a flame photometer[10]. Cornwall (1958) discusses methods for quantifying the amounts of gypsum, silica and nitrogen present in a sample, together with a wide range of spot tests for identifying the presence of various substances. Hardan (1971) discusses the results of a project measuring soil salinity, in the Lower Mesopotamian plain. This area had been under irrigation for several millennia and the soils are alluvial. Soil salinity is one of the main factors limiting agricultural development, and there is evidence from the ancient records that it was a similar problem in the period 2400–2100 B C

Hardan studies a series of samples obtained from the sun-dried mud bricks of the area, incorporated into buildings and probably manufactured from soils near the building sites. He selected four sites on the Tigris valley and an additional four from the valley of the Euphrates. Measurements were taken of the chloride/sulphate ratio, and the amount of calcium carbonate and gypsum present, using the methods developed by the US Salinity Laboratory. By correlating the results obtained with archaeological dates, he showed that the soils of the area were both saline and alkaline *before* the development of agriculture or the inception of irrigation at 7000–6000 B C. This conclusion refutes a previous hypothesis that irrigation of the area was the direct cause of its salinity, and provides an interesting example of the archaeological dating of sedimentological processes.

References

BIEK, L. (1960). 'Appendix 1. The soils in Craig-a-merrin: a Bronze Age barrow at Liskey, Cornwall', *Proceedings of the Prehistoric Society*, **26**, 76–98

BROWN, G. and OLLIER, C. D. (1956). 'Collophane from the chalk', *Mineralogical Magazine*, **31**, 339–343

BRUNELLE, R. L., HOFFMAN, C. M., SNOW, K. B. and PRO, M. J. (1969). 'Neutron activation and atomic absorption analyses of chemical elements in soils', *Journal of the Association of Analytical Chemists*, **52** (5), 911–914

CATT, J. A. and WEIR, A. H. (1975). 'The study of archaeologically important sediments by petrological techniques', in *Geoarchaeology: Earth Science and the Past*, ed. Davidson, D. A. and Shackley, M. L. (Duckworth, London)

CORNWALL, I. W. (1958). *Soils for the Archaeologist* (Phoenix, London)

CORNWALL, I. W. (1959). 'Appendix 3. Report on the soil samples in the excavation of a long barrow at Nutbane, Hants.', *Proceedings of the Prehistoric Society*, **25**, 15–52

CORNWALL, I. W. (1960). 'Appendix 2. Soil samples from the Druid's circle', *Proceedings of the Prehistoric Society*, **26**, 303–340

COOK, S. F. and HEITZER, R. F. (1965). 'Studies on the chemical analysis of archaeological sites' (University of California Publication in Anthropology, Los Angeles)

DAUNCEY, K. D. M. (1952). 'Phosphate content of soils in archaeological sites 1', *The Advancement of Science*, **9**, 33–36

DAVIDSON, D. A. (1973). 'Particle size and phosphate analysis—evidence for the evolution of a tell', *Archaeometry*, **15** (1), 143–152

GRANT GOSS, M. (1971). 'Carbon determination', in *Procedures in Sedimentary Petrology*, ed. Carver, R. (Wiley, New York)

GROVES, A. W. (1951). *Silicate Analysis* (London)

GUNDLACH, H. (1961). *Tüpfelmethode auf Phosphat angewandt in Praehistorischer Forschung in Mikrochemika Acta*, **5** (196), 735–737

HARDAN, A. (1971). 'Archaeological methods for dating soil salinity in the Mesopotamian plain', in *Paleopedology*, ed. Yaalon, D. H. (International Society of Soil Science and Israel University Press, Jerusalem)

HESSE, P. R. (1971). *A Textbook of Soil Chemical Analysis* (Chemical Publishing, New York)

JACKSON, M. L. (1962). *Soil Chemical Analysis* (Prentice-Hall, London)

LAVILLE, H. (1975). 'The fill of rock shelters; methods of analysis and climatic interpretation', in *Geoarchaeology: Earth Science and the Past*, ed. Davidson, D. A. and Shackley, M. L. (Duckworth, London)

LAVILLE, H., NIKITINE, S. and THIBAULT, C. (1969). 'Etude geologique du remplissage de la grotte de Chazelles', *Quaternaria*, **11**, 161–188

LORSCH, W. (1940). 'Die siedlungsgeographische Phosphatmethode', *Die Naturwissenschaften*, **40–41**, 633–640

LOUIS, M. (1946). 'Methodes des phosphates', *Cahiers d'histoire et d'archaeologie*, 119–120

LUTZ, H. G. (1951). 'Concentrations of certain chemical elements in soils of Alaskan archaeological sites', *American Journal of Science*, **249**, 925–928

MATTINGLY, G. E. and WILSON, R. J. (1962). 'A note on the chemical analysis of a soil buried since Roman times', *Journal of Soil Science*, **13** (2), 254–259

VAN MOORT, J. C. and DE VRIES, D. (1970). 'Rapid carbon determination by dry combustion in soil science and geochemistry', *Geoderma*, **4** (2), 109–118

MUIR, J. W. (1952). 'The determinance of total phosphorus in soils, with particular reference to the control of interference by soluble silica', *Analyst*, **77**, 313–317

MÜLLER, G. and GASTNER, M. (1971). 'The "Karbonat-Bombe"—a simple device for the determination of the carbonate content in sediments, soils and other materials', *Neus. Jb. Miner. Mh.*, **10**, 466–469

MULVANEY, D. J. and JOYCE, E. B. (1965). 'Archaeological and geomorphological investigations on Mount Moffatt, Queensland, Australia', *Proceedings of the Prehistoric Society*, **31**, 147–213

MURPHY, J. and RILEY, J. P. (1962). 'A modified single method for the determination of phosphate in natural waters', *Analytica Chemica Acta*, **27**, 31–36

PROUDFOOT, V. B. (1975). 'Phosphate determinations, significance of results and interpretation of sites in podzolic environments', in *Geoarchaeology: Earth Science and the Past*, ed. Davidson, D. A. and Shackley, M. L. (Duckworth, London)

PROVAN, D. (1971). 'Soil phosphate analysis as a tool in archaeology', *Norwegian Archaeological Reviews*, **4**, 37–50

ROSENFELD, A. (1966). 'Analysis of residual deposits associated with interments', *Proceedings of the Prehistoric Society*, **32**, 142–143

SCHWARTZ, G. T. (1967). 'Prospecting without a computer in southern Switzerland', *Estratto da Prospezioni Archaeologische*, **2**, 73–80

SHUKLA, G. C. and SINGH, M. (1968). 'Photo-electric colorimetric method for estimation of nitrogen in soil', *Journal of the Indian Society for Soil Science*, **16** (1), 77–81

SIEVEKING, G. DE G., BUSH, P., FERGUSON, J., CRADDOCK, P. T., HUGHES, M. J. and COWELL, M. R. (1972). 'Prehistoric flint mines and their identification as sources of raw material', *Archaeometry*, **14** (2), 151–176

SOKOLOFF, V. P. and CARTER, G. F. (1952). 'Time and trace metals in archaeological sites', *Science*, **116**, 1–5

STEWARD, J. H. and OADES, J. M. (1972). 'The determination of organic phosphorus in soils', *Journal of Soil Science*, **23** (1), 38–50

TITE, M. S. (1973). *Methods of Physical Examination in Archaeology* (Seminar Press, London)

WALKELY, A. and BLACK, D. C. (1934). 'An examination of the Degtjareeff method for determining soil organic matter, and a proposed modification of the chromic acid titration method', *Soil Science*, **37**, 29–38

WARD, F. N., NAKAGAWA, H. M., HARMS, T. F. and VAN SICKLE, G. (1969). 'Atomic-absorption methods of analysis useful in geochemical exploration', *Bulletin of the US Geological Survey*, 1289

WEST, T. S. (1971). 'Versatile atomic fluorescence spectroscopy', *Chemistry in Britain*, **7** (9), 378–388

Chapter 7

MICROSCOPE TECHNIQUES

The use of a microscope provides a means for observing, describing and analysing the visible characteristics of sediments. These are so important that the majority of soil classifications are made on visual grounds—for example, those of Kubiena (1935). At an early stage in description a hand lens may be used to make observations about the fabric, texture and particle types composing the sediment, which can later be expanded by using techniques involving a stereoscopic or polarising microscope. Low-power examination of sediments is a valuable tool for the identification of particles that do not form a fundamental part of the structure of the sediment, such as included grains of industrial, faunal or archaeological material. The identification of such inclusions may be done by spreading the dry sediment out on a sheet of contrasting colour and examining it under low magnification, using incident light. For a more sophisticated analysis, perhaps involving a particle size or shape quantification, the sediment may be mounted to facilitate inspection, as either a thin section or a loose grain mount (p. 52). If the sediment is soft, it must first be impregnated with some suitable medium before a thin section can be cut.

MICROSCOPE TYPES

Since the questions posed during a visual sediment inspection tend to be varied and since individual instruments have their limitations, it may often be necessary to employ several different varieties of microscope. The microscope may occasionally need to be linked to a device for automated recording, such as the electromagnetic counter bank (*Figure 11.1*, p. 138), or an instrument for projecting the image or photographing it. The major optical companies manufacture different types of microscopes for different purposes, with wide ranges of accessories, and working details may be readily obtained on application to the company concerned.

COMPOUND MICROSCOPES

For more detailed work at higher magnifications a more sophisticated instrument than the hand lens is required. The compound microscope

(*Figure 7.1*) includes a condenser, and an ocular (eyepiece). The condenser collects the light and projects it into the plane of the specimen. The objective projects the illuminated specimen image into the intermediate image plane (*Figure 7.1*), and the ocular acts like a hand magnifier to add a second magnification stage for the human eye. Numerous different types

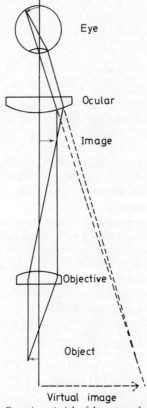

Fig. 7.1. *Operating principle of the compound microscope*

of objectives are manufactured at standard magnifications, although the final size of the image is controlled by both the focal length of the objective and the magnification of the eyepiece. The magnification of the objective can be obtained from the formula:

$$M = l/f$$

where M = magnification of the objective; l = tube length (distance between the upper end of the objective and the upper end of the eyepiece); and f = focal length of the objective (as marked on the eyepiece). The total magnification (in diameters) of the objective and the eyepiece is found from the formula:

$$X = \frac{l}{f} \times e$$

where X = total magnification and e = magnification of the eyepiece (as marked). *Table 7.1* lists values for the total magnification for different eyepiece magnifications and different objective focal lengths. Objectives are best mounted on a rotary holder on the instrument which centres automatically and permits of easy magnification change. Eyepieces for

Table 7.1 TO FIND THE TOTAL MAGNIFICATION OF AN OBJECT

Focal length of objective (f)		Magnification of eyepiece (e)						
in	mm	×4	×5	×6	×8	×10	×12	×15
2	50	13	16	19	26	32	38	48
1	25	26	32	38	51	64	76	96
$\frac{2}{3}$	16	40	50	60	80	100	120	150
$\frac{1}{3}$	8	80	100	120	160	200	240	300
$\frac{1}{4}$	6	106	133	160	213	266	319	399
$\frac{1}{6}$	4	160	200	240	320	400	480	600
$\frac{1}{8}$	3	212	265	318	424	530	636	795
$\frac{1}{12}$	2	320	400	480	640	800	960	1200
$\frac{1}{15}$	1.7	376	470	564	752	940	1128	1410

compound microscopes are available in a wide range of magnifications from ×4 to at least ×30, although this obviously varies with the microscope model. The more precise (and expensive) the optical system of the microscope the greater the accuracy of the image magnification obtained. The condenser, located under the specimen stage, provides a converging cone of light to illuminate the specimen, and is combined with a mirror and a sub-stage iris diaphragm, and sometimes with a polariser.

The use of a *stereomicroscope* such as the Wild M5 shown in *Figure 7.2* enables the object, perhaps the individual grains of a sediment, to be viewed in three dimensions, by using two separate objective–eyepiece systems which produce two separate images, each from a slightly different viewing angle. This technique gives a larger field of view and a longer working distance. Magnifications range from ×6 to ×50, although this may sometimes be extended to ×1.5–×200; above this the three-dimensional effect is lost. The instrument is particularly useful for sediment examination and for particle description, since it can be used with either incident or transmitted light. Pale sediments should be viewed on a dark ground with incident light, using an oblique light source that is either fixed to the instrument or free-standing. Particle shapes can easily be measured and described, either mounted on a slide or loose, a transparent specimen stage and transmitted light being used. Most models of stereomicroscope have a large range of accessories, including polarisers, rotary stages and attachments for photography. The Wild model is especially useful since it is light and easily portable and incorporates semi-automatic magnification change[17]. *Figure 7.2* shows the optical system, set for operation with an incident light source. If the instrument is being used on low power for sample examination, incident light and a contrasting background are

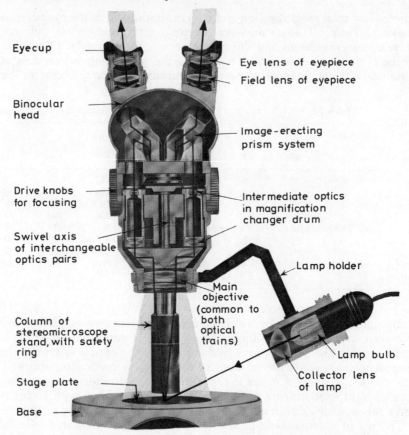

Eyecup

Eye lens of eyepiece

Field lens of eyepiece

Binocular head

Image-erecting prism system

Drive knobs for focusing

Intermediate optics in magnification changer drum

Swivel axis of interchangeable optics pairs

Lamp holder

Main objective (common to both optical trains)

Column of stereomicroscope stand, with safety ring

Lamp bulb

Collector lens of lamp

Stage plate

Base

Fig. 7.2. Optical system of the Wild M5 Stereomicroscope. (Reproduced by courtesy of Wild Ltd)

required; but if a slide is being examined, the use of a rotary stage and transmitted light from a source in the microscope base is necessary.

PARTICLE IDENTIFICATION
(using a hand lens or stereomicroscope)

The identification of 'foreign' particles in a sediment is one of the most important steps in analysis, since the matter included in a sediment is often as diagnostic as the sediment itself and may provide vital clues to depositional history. The writer has extracted pieces of Medieval textile from a supposedly *in situ* natural clay sample at the base of a ditch, diagnostic fragments of early Medieval pottery from an otherwise archaeologically sterile layer, important insect remains from a fine-grained Pleistocene sand, and lead nodules and imported fossils from cave sediments (Shackley, 1973), by examining samples under a stereomicroscope.

It is obviously impossible to give a guide to all the particles that might be met with in the course of an analysis, although an indication of some chemical and physical tests to identify their composition might be helpful. It is a good practice to carry out a simple visual examination as part of standard laboratory characterisation, and the results may conveniently be recorded on the initial work-sheet (*Figure 3.1*, p. 34). Few people are capable of memorising the shapes, characteristics and tests for every type of particle, and constant reference must be made to charts, tables or standard collections.

PARTICLE REFERENCE SETS

The use of particle reference standards, as mounted slides, charts or tables, is a valuable research aid and has been much favoured in various industrial fields. Perhaps the most significant development in recent years has been the publication of the 'Particle Atlas' (McCrone and Delly, 1973), which includes details and drawings for the identification of thousands of different types of particles[13]. McCrone Ltd[13] also manufacture particle reference sets which accompany the Atlas, and include organic, inorganic, fibrous and industrial particles mounted on slides. Cutrock Engineering Ltd[6] produce mineral and crystal reference sets, and the Greer Drug Corporation market over 200 varieties of pollen and other materials, both as slides and in powder form. The R.P. Cargille Lab. Inc. market sets of metal and industrial particles, including minerals, petrographic specimens, furs,

Table 7.2 HINTS FOR THE IDENTIFICATION OF ORGANIC PARTICLES
(qualitative tests)

Test	Result	Indications
(1) Moisten with 0.1N I_2 in 0.4N KI solution	(a) Turns blue	(a) Starch, plant tissues?
	(b) Turns yellow or brown	(b) Protein, fat, oil, wool, silk
	(c) Turns brown, then blue after some time	(c) Artificial cellulose (check for sample contamination)
(2) Moisten with HNO_3 and heat till dry	(a) Turns yellow	(a) Protein
(3) Moisten with a solution of 1g phloroglucinol in 50 ml ethanol which has been treated with 25 ml HCl	(a) Turns red	(a) Lignin. Wood tissue
(4) Add hot dilute NaOH solution and boil	(a) Turns brown	(a) Humus
(5) Substance appears as a black powder. Burn in air	(a) Turns red on burning, leaving white ash	(a) Carbon. Carbonised grain, seeds, charcoal?

hairs and fibres, together with sets of crystals, minerals and glasses for refractive index standards. Firth sells biological specimens, especially diatoms, and other collections of organic materials are sold by the major drug houses and equipment suppliers. The major national museums also have immensely valuable collections of specimens, including slides and photographs, and are usually pleased to assist with problem particles if given a little notice.

Table 7.2 presents some of the standard tests for the identification of organic particles, and *Table 7.3* the tests for identifying the most commonly occurring inorganic substances.

Table 7.3 HINTS FOR THE IDENTIFICATION OF INORGANIC PARTICLES
(qualitative tests)

Test	Result	Indications
(1) White powder. Add H_2O	(a) Dissolves (b) Dissolves, giving strongly alkaline solution (c) Dissolves and will turn litmus blue (d) Dissolves and turns phenolphthalein magenta	(a) Gypsum? Salt? (b) Borax, sodium carbonate? (c) Borax (d) Sodium carbonate
(2) White powder. Add HCl	(a) Effervescence of CO_2 (b) Insoluble (c) Slight effervescence of CO_2. Substance dissolves in mineral acids	(a) Carbonates. Chalk? Limestone? Plaster? (b) Calcium sulphate gypsum? (c) Calcium phosphate bone ash?
(3) White powder. Add 2 drops solution ammonium molybdate with H_2SO_4, then 2 drops ascorbic acid solution	(a) Blue colour	(a) Phosphates
(4) Black powder. Add conc. HCl	(a) Yellow colour (b) Greenish-yellow colour which fades if H_2O added	(a) Iron oxide (b) Manganese oxide
(5) Black powder. Add H_2O	(a) Blue-black solution	(a) Iron tannates (ink)
(6) Black powder. Ignite	(a) Red-brown colour	(a) Ferrous oxide
(7) Black powder. Add dilute acid	(a) Smell of H_2S (bad eggs)	(a) Sulphides
(8) Brown/yellow powder. Add conc. HCl	(a) Effervescence	(a) Ferric oxide? Ferric carbonate?
(9) Red powder. Add conc. HCl	(a) Yellow solution	(a) Burnt brick? Burnt clay? Iron-rich soil?
(10) Green/blue powder—try copper salts or minerals. If accompanying damp bone, it is probably vivianite		
(11) Pink powders—try manganese or iron compounds, or feldspars		
(12) Heat with acid on a clean platinum wire	(a) Brick-red colour	(a) Calcium
(13) Borax bead tests. Add HNO_3 and heat on platinum wire	(a) Green colour (b) Emerald-green colour	(a) Chromium (b) Copper

Test	Result	Indications
(14) Heat with charcoal, moisten with cobalt nitrate and reheat strongly	(a) Fused blue mass (b) Unfused blue mass (c) Pink residue (d) Grass-green colour	(a) Phosphate (b) Aluminium (c) Magnesium (d) Zinc
(15) Borax bead test	(a) Yellow colour when hot, green when cold, in oxidising flame	(a) Iron
(16) Heat with KI and S	(a) Bright yellow crust	(a) Lead
(17) Heat on charcoal with KI and S	(a) Greenish-yellow crust and fumes	(a) Mercury
(18) Borax bead test	(a) Red-brown in oxidising flame, grey in reducing flame	(a) Nickel
(19) Heat on potassium wire with acid	(a) Violet (b) Yellow	(a) Potassium (b) Sodium

PETROLOGICAL MICROSCOPE

A petrological microscope with a polariser is essential for the detailed study of soil or sediment structures, and for the optical identification of minerals. Minerals are identified on the basis of their crystal form, cleavage, colour, pleochroism and extinction angles, and the process is both highly skilled and time-consuming. Helpful techniques are described by Hubert (1971), Milner (1962) and Boswell (1933), but expert tuition is required. Rosenfeld (1965) has made a detailed study of many of the minerals and rocks that occur in archaeological contexts, and the optical system of the petrological microscope and the basis of mineral identification is discussed by Tite (1972).

HEAVY MINERAL ANALYSIS

The heavy mineral content of a sediment or rock is particularly diagnostic of its provenance, a fact that has been applied to archaeological ceramics by Peacock (1967, 1970). The heavy minerals, with specific gravities greater than 2.9, may be used to identify the parent material of a sediment, by noting the presence and relative abundance of certain mineral types. Less weathered materials tend to have a greater variety of heavy minerals. There is, however, a close relationship between the heavy mineral assemblage and the sediment grain size, and two sediment samples drawn from the same source with identical depositional histories will have different heavy mineral contents if the sediment grain size is not the same. This occurs because all sizes of a heavy mineral suite do not occur with equal abundance (Carver, 1971). It is usual to study only one size fraction, generally the very fine sand, although Müller (1967) recommends examination of the 63 μm–200 μm range. Krumbein and Rasmussen (1941) made a study of sources of error in heavy mineral studies, examining the 124–175 μm and 175–246 μm fractions of sediments separately, and found that the sampling and laboratory errors were lower for the coarse fraction.

PREPARATION OF SAMPLES

In order to prepare a heavy mineral suite for identification, the sample must first be pre-treated; secondly, the heavy and light mineral fractions must be separated off; and the heavy minerals must then be mounted and identified. The dry sample may be crushed in a pestle and mortar (not ground), and the appropriate size fraction removed by sieving.

The splitting of a mineral assemblage into heavy and light fractions is usually accomplished by the 'sink or float' technique in which the different components are separated off in a heavy liquid of a prescribed density. The less dense minerals will float and the denser will sink. The heavy mineral fraction usually forms less than 2–3% of the total minerals present, except in highly ferruginous sediments or rocks. The reagents most frequently used are S-tetrabromoethane (specific gravity 2.95–3) or bromoform (specific gravity 2.88–2.90). Both are colourless and have characteristic smells. Bromoform is less viscous than tetrabromoethane, but also more volatile. A sample of the sediment is added to the heavy liquid in a separating funnel and left to stand. The heavy minerals separate out and may be collected, washed and mounted in loose grain mounts using Canada Balsam (p. 52). The heavy liquid is recovered and recycled. The whole process is described by Hubert (1971).

PREPARATION OF THIN SECTIONS

Thin sections have long been used to characterise and distinguish the rock types of artifacts, glacial erratics and other material which occur in archaeological contexts, as well as for obtaining the provenance of ceramics (Peacock, 1967). The study of unconsolidated sediments in thin section gives a great deal of information on micromorphology and microfabric, and is particularly useful in the characterisation of palaeosols. The thin section may be used for mineralogical identification and quantification of particle size and shape, and for description of textural characteristics. It can yield information on texture, fabric, mineral and fossil content and sediment diagenesis.

Different sets of techniques are required for preparing thin sections from consolidated and unconsolidated materials, since the latter must be impregnated before they can be cut. The following equipment is required:

Apparatus
Power grinding machine[16]
Plate glass lap for hand grinding

Glass specimen slides and coverslips
Hot plate
Forceps, labels, etc.

Chemicals
Grinding abrasives (Carborundum 400,3F and 600, Aloxite 600)
Mounting media (Canada Balsam, Lakeside 70, Permount, Araldite)
Cleaning or diluting chemicals (xylene, toluene, paraffin)
Grinding fluids (water or paraffin)
Cover fluids (glycerine, Permount, clear nail varnish)
Impregnating media (Araldite, Canada Balsam, etc.).

THIN SECTIONS OF ROCKS

The thickness of a good thin section should be 30 μm, where quartz will show grey to yellow interference colours when viewed under the microscope. If the material is sufficiently hard to be cut and ground without breaking, then it need not be impregnated. This is often the case with very cemented materials such as cave breccias. A thin chip is required, 1–2 in square, which is cut with a power wheel[6]. The method is as follows:

(1) Grind one side of the chip flat with a grooved lap wheel (preferably diamond-surfaced), using either water or paraffin as a grinding fluid, depending on whether the sediment is water-soluble. Slight pressure is needed.
(2) Clean and prepare a 3×1 in microscope slide and cement the chip to it with the ground face downwards.
(3) After the cementing medium has fully hardened, the other face of the chip must be ground to a uniform thickness of 30 μm. Coarse grinding is carried out on the power wheel to a thickness of about 1 mm, and the slide is then transferred to a glass plate and ground with successively finer abrasives in a slurry made with either water or paraffin. Hand grinding is carried out using a circular motion and light pressure, keeping the finger tips well out of the way.
(4) The specimen must be periodically examined under a petrological microscope to gauge when the correct thickness has been achieved. The slide is then clearly labelled and the procedure and chemicals used are noted in the laboratory notebook.
(5) The thin section may be covered by a glass coverslip if necessary, or protected by spraying with acrylic plastics. Excess cement may be cleaned off with toluene, and care must be taken to remove all small particles of the abrasive by washing with the appropriate fluid, a natural sponge or linen cloth being used to remove persistent particles.

It is not always necessary to use a coverglass, although generally recommended. The coverglass may be a nuisance if any chemical tests are required at a later date; although if this is allowed for during the manufacture of a slide, the appropriate portions can be blocked off and protected with masking tape (Ireland, 1971).

CEMENTING MEDIA

Various commercial products are available for cementing the chip to the slide. *Lakeside 70*[6] is an excellent cement, since it adheres very strongly to glass. It has a refractive index of 1.54 and a melting point of about 140 °C. The slide needs to be heated on a laboratory hot plate to the required temperature and a little of the material melted on to it. Lakeside 70 is produced in a stick. The ground face of the chip is then pressed on to the hot plate (paper-covered) for a few seconds before being pressed firmly on to the cement-covered end of the slide, which is then removed from the hot plate. *Canada Balsam* may also be used for mounting, the same procedures being observed as those already described for mounting loose grains (p. 52). *Permount* is not recommended as a cement for the chip, since it takes so long to dry, but it has the advantage of not forming bubbles, since it does not require heating. A few drops are spread on the slide and the chip pressed on. The slide must then be left for some weeks before the medium is hard enough for final grinding. Another suitable cementing medium is *Araldite*, as a mixture of either Araldite E with Araldite hardener 951, in the ratio 100:11, or Araldite E with hardener 943, in the ratio 100:20. The cement and hardener are mixed in the correct proportions with a disposable spatula on a piece of cardboard before being transferred to the slide. The chip is then pressed firmly down and left for at least 24 h (Müller, 1967).

IMPREGNATION OF UNCONSOLIDATED SEDIMENTS

If the sediment is too friable to stand cutting and grinding, it must first be impregnated. Several suitable methods are available. *Carbowax*, a waxlike polyethylene glycol, is particularly suitable for impregnating moist sediments, especially clays. Carbowax 4000 is soluble in water and melts at 55 °C. The lump of sediment must be left in a small beaker of melted wax in an oven for about 3 days at 60 °C. It is then removed, left to dry and ground and mounted as above. Grinding must be carried out in xylene or toluene. *Canada Balsam* is a suitable medium for impregnating soft fine sediments, and Waldo and Tester (1937) describe a method for using it in a vacuum, which improves penetration. The standard method consists of immersing the sediment lump until it hardens, before allowing it to dry and mounting it in the usual way.

Cornwall (1958) discusses the use of *Dammar gum* for impregnation, since it becomes thin and mobile at 150 °C and will penetrate even the finest sediments. It has the disadvantage of not adhering well to glass. *Lakeside 70* may also be used, and is most efficient when combined with an equal volume of a 50/50 mixture of alcohol and acetone to act as a solvent. Impregnation with *Araldite* gives better results than with any other medium with very fine sediments, although the process is very slow, taking a week for each sample.

INTERPRETATION OF THIN SECTIONS

Much geological literature is available about sediment micromorphology and interpretations that may be made from thin sections of sediments, and several recent papers apply the techniques to archaeological problems. Proudfoot (1969) used thin sections as an aid to the characterisation of soil samples from the Early Bronze Age stone row at Cholwichton in Devon. He suggested on the basis of evidence provided by thin sections and ignition tests that the site had been built in an area of open heathland vegetation rather than woodland. Examination of the sections showed brown pellets that might represent faecal material, and also enabled a detailed character-isation of the Bronze Age soil profile to be made. The same writer under-took a detailed microscopic analysis of thin sections taken from a soil series through the bank of a henge monument at Nunwich, Yorks. (Proud-foot, 1963). Here a buried soil was identified as a brownearth whose top layers were undergoing leaching and gradually attaining the fabric charac-teristics of the illuvial horizon of a podsolic brown earth (Kubiena, 1958). The soil evidence permitted of the reconstruction of a series of events commencing with the formation of the brownearth on the silts of an old river flood plain. This soil was then gently leached and the bank of the henge monument constructed on top of it. The topsoil and the bank material were then subjected to further leaching and ploughing.

The analysis of a soil in thin section is undoubtedly the best way of characterising its profile. Soil formation implies a period of relative stability when little erosion of old material or deposition of new sediments was taking place. Soil profiles change in response to factors such as the forma-tion of humus or the movement of very fine material through the profile, and these can be noted in thin section (Catt and Weir, 1975; Cornwall, 1958). Kubiena (1935, 1963, 1970) and Dalrymple (1958) quote examples of the use of micromorphological examination of buried soils in thin section, to reconstruct past environmental conditions, and Federoff (1967, 1968, 1969) and Jamagne (1972) discuss the interpretation of soil thin sections as palaeoclimatic indicators.

References

BOSWELL, P. H. G. (1933). *Mineralogy of Sedimentary Rocks* (Murby, London)
CARVER, R. (1971). 'Heavy mineral separations', in *Procedures in Sedimentary Petrology*, ed. Carver, R. (Wiley, New York)
CATT, J. A. and WEIR, A. H. (1975). 'The study of archaeologically important sediments by petro-graphic techniques', in *Geoarchaeology: Earth Science and the Past*, ed. Davidson, D. A. and Shackley, M. L. (Duckworth, London)
CORNWALL, I. W. (1958). *Soils for the Archaeologist* (Phoenix, London)

DALRYMPLE, J. B. (1958). 'The application of soil micromorphology to fossil soils and other deposits from archaeological sites', *Journal of Soil Science*, **9**, 199–209

FEDEROFF, N. (1967). 'Un example d'application de la micromorphologie à l'étude des palaesols', *Bull. Assn. fr. Etude Quaternaire*, **3**, 193–209

FEDEROFF, N. (1968). 'Analyses morphologie de sols à horizon B textural en France Atlantique', *Sci Sol*, **1**, 29–65

FEDEROFF, N. (1969). 'Caractères micromorphologiques des pedogeneses quaternaires en France' in *Etudes sur le Quaternaire dans le Monde (8th INQUA Congress, Paris, 1969)*, 341–349

HUBERT, J. F. (1971). 'Analysis of heavy mineral assemblages', in *Procedures in Sedimentary Petrology*, ed. Carver, R. (Wiley, New York)

IRELAND, H. A. (1971). 'Preparation of thin sections', in *Procedures in Sedimentary Petrology*, ed. Carver, R. (Wiley, New York)

JAMAGNE, M. (1972). 'Some micromorphological aspects of soils developed in loess deposits of northern France', in *Soil Micromorphology (Proc. 3rd. Int. Working Meeting, Wroclaw, Poland, 1969)*, 559–582

KRUMBEIN, W. C. and RASMUSSEN, W. C. (1941). 'The probable error of sampling beach sand for heavy mineral analysis', *Journal of Sedimentary Petrology*, **11**, 10–20

KUBIENA, W. L. (1953). *The Soils of Europe* (Murby, London)

KUBIENA, W. L. (1963). 'Palaeosols as indicators of palaeoclimates', *Arid. Zone Research*, **20**, 207–209

KUBIENA, W. L. (1970). *Micromorphological Features of Soil Geography* (Rutgers University Press, New Brunswick)

MCCRONE, W. and DELLY, J. G. (1973). *The Particle Atlas* (Ann Arbor Science, Michigan)

MILNER, H. B. (1962). *Sedimentary Petrography*, 2nd ed. (Allen and Unwin, New York/London)

MÜLLER, G. (1967). *Methods in Sedimentary Petrology* (Hafner, Stuttgart)

PEACOCK, D. P. S. (1967). 'The heavy mineral analysis of pottery: a preliminary report', *Archaeometry*, **10**, 97–100

PEACOCK, D. P. S. (1970). 'The scientific analysis of ancient ceramics: a review', *World Archaeology*, **1**, 375–389

PROUDFOOT, V. B. (1963). 'Soil report on the henge monument at Nunwich', *Yorkshire Archaeological Journal*, **161**, 41 (1), 103–107

PROUDFOOT, V. B. (1969). 'Soil report on samples from Cholwichton Stone Row', *Proceedings of the Prehistoric Society*, **35**, 217–219

SHACKLEY, M. L. (1973). 'The Alveston bone fissure' (with H. Taylor), *Proceedings of the University of Bristol Speleological Society*, **13** (2), 135–152

ROSENFELD, A. (1965). *The Inorganic Raw Materials of Antiquity* (Weidenfeld and Nicholson, London)

TITE, M. S. (1972). *Methods of Physical Examination in Archaeology* (Seminar Press, London)

WALDO, A. W. and TESTER, S. T. (1937). 'Methods of impregnating porous materials to facilitate pore studies', *Bull. Am. Assoc. Petrol. Geologists*, **21**, 259–267

Chapter 8

PARTICLE SIZE ANALYSIS

PRINCIPLES

SIGNIFICANCE OF PARTICLE SIZE

Undertaking a particle size analysis of a sediment is without doubt the most useful way of obtaining detailed information about the characteristics of the sediment and of describing them. Accurate completion of such analyses and the correct plotting and interpretation of results enable samples to be described in terms of statistical measures, permitting of direct correlations between similar deposits, stratigraphic units or sediments that have been produced or influenced by similar sets of processes. Particle size analysis should permit of the detection of the *agent* of deposition (for example, wind, river, sea), the *process* of deposition (for example, suspension, saltation) and the *environment* of deposition (for example, beach, flood plain, dune). In some cases factors which have affected the sediment *in situ* (for example, weathering) can also be detected. A particle size distribution is therefore an invaluable aid in sediment characterisation, and should ideally be combined with further tests—for example, an examination of grain surface textures—for a complete sediment description. It is impossible to describe the composition or texture of a sediment, or to classify it, unless an accurate particle size distribution has been carried out.

Before an analysis is attempted, it is important to understand exactly what is meant by the term 'particle size'. The type of particle size analysis undertaken on a particular sediment depends on the following factors: (1) the desired measurement of particle 'size'; (2) the likely range of sizes to be measured; (3) the required degree of accuracy; and (4) the available equipment, money and time.

There are dozens of methods available for obtaining a particle size distribution, but the success of each is dependent on a good understanding of the theoretical processes governing the method, and on a reliably selected and correctly prepared sample. Casually passing a lump of sediment through a series of sieves and expressing the results on a piece of graph paper is worse than useless, since it may be deliberately misleading. Each stage of the process needs to be carefully reasoned and understood, and it is for this reason that, although the final size distribution is an immense source of potential information, its interpretation must be made with caution unless the correct procedures and a certain degree of care have been applied in obtaining it.

DEFINITIONS OF PARTICLE SIZE

All methods of measuring particle size are empirical, because 'size' cannot be defined except for geometrically simple shapes, and even for these the chosen analytical method influences the results. For example a tube-shaped particle ⊂⊃ has the 'size' O in a sieve analysis, but the size ▭

Table 8.1   MEASUREMENTS OF PARTICLE 'SIZE'

Method of measurement	Commonly used symbol	Name	Definition
Sieving	d_A	Sieve diameter	The width of the minimum square aperture through which the particle will pass
Sedimentation	d_f	Free-falling diameter	The diameter of a sphere having the same density and the same free-falling speed as the particle in a fluid of the same density and viscosity
	d_{St}	Stokes's diameter	The free-falling diameter in the laminar flow region
Microscopy	d_{ns}	Nominal sectional diameter	The diameter of a circle of the same area as the grain projection (Wadell, 1935)
Microscopy	Optical statistical diameters	Martin's diameter	The length of the line which divides the projected area of the grain into two equal parts (Martin, 1926)
		Feret's diameter	The maximum projected length of the grain size on a fixed line (Feret, 1931)
		Maximum horizontal intercept	The maximum length of a line parallel to a fixed direction limited by the contours of the grain (Krumbein, 1935)
		Longest dimension	A measured value equal to the maximum value of Feret's diameter for each particle

if it is being examined under a microscope. Similarly, the two spheres ◎ O, of the same diameter, are defined as being of the same 'size' under a microscope but of different 'sizes' in sedimentation analysis. Studies of size distributions usually relate the size of the particles being examined to an equivalent spherical dimension or diameter, i.e. to the diameter of a spherical particle whose volume is equal to that of the particle whose size is being measured (Rosen and Hulbert, 1970), but many other definitions of size are also employed (Heywood, 1947).

A spherical particle may be characterised by its diameter, and a cube by the length of one edge, similar processes being employed for other regularly shaped particles. However, the majority of mineral grains are far from regular in form, and may be platy, needle-like or amorphous. They may even consist of aggregates of smaller particles. This presents problems in measurement (Pietsch, 1968). The particle size being measured is totally dependent upon the method employed, and there is a significant lack of appreciation of the influence of technique on results (Littlejohn, 1970).

Table 8.1 presents a summary of some of the most commonly used definitions of particle size, which are shown diagrammatically in *Figure 8.1*.

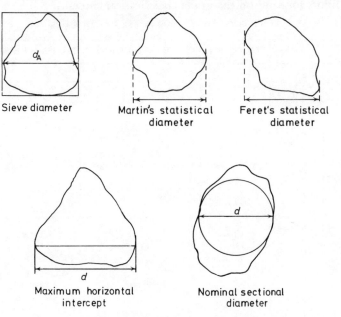

Fig. 8.1. Definitions of particle 'size'

The relationships between certain of these measurements have been discussed by Heywood (1946), and between the optical statistical diameters and the sieve diameter by Krumbein (1935), Chayes (1949), Friedman (1962) and Van der Plas (1962). Direct comparison of results obtained from different sizing methods may not always be possible, and this presents a complication if a compound particle size distribution curve has to be drawn. The most commonly used combination of methods, sieving and sedimentation, measures two different particle 'sizes', and the combination of results obtained will produce a distinct 'kink' in the size distribution curve. However, both these methods produce a volume or weight/size distribution, whereas optical sizing usually results in a number/size distribution, since individual particles are measured. The two systems may be interconverted (p. 135).

SIZE GRADES

Although all the particles composing the sediment differ from one another only by very small size gradations along a continuum, it is convenient to group them into size grades, distinguished on fairly arbitrary criteria. These 'grades' refer only to the particle size of the sediment, and are not related in any way to its mineralogical composition. Thus, a 'sand' may be composed of particles of coal or calcite instead of the more usual quartz, so long as the predominant particle size falls within the grade limits for sand on the grade classification chosen.

Table 8.2 SCALES FOR PARTICLE SIZE ANALYSIS

d_A(mm)	ϕ scale	Udden (1914)	Wentworth (1922)	British Standard
64	−6		Cobbles	Cobbles
45.3	−5.5	Boulders		
32	−5			
22.6	−4.5		Pebbles	Gravel
16.0	−4			
11.2	−3.5			
8.0	−3	Gravel		
5.65	−2.5			
4.00	−2			
2.82	−1.5		Granules	
2.00	−1			
1.41	−0.5	Coarse	V. coarse	Coarse
1.00	0			
700 μm	+0.5	Medium		
500	+1	Sand	Coarse	Sand
354	+1.5	Fine	Sand	
251	+2		Medium	Medium
178	+2.5	V. fine		
124	+3		Fine	
88	+3.5	V. coarse		Fine
62	+4		V. fine	
44	+4.5	Coarse		Coarse
31	+5	Silt		
22	+5.5	Fine	Silt	Silt
16	+6			Medium
11	+6.5	V. fine		
7.8	+7			
5.5	+7.5	V. coarse		
3.9	+8	Clay		Fine
2.8	+8.5	Coarse	Clay	
2	+9			
1.4	+9.5	Fine		Clay

The distribution of particle sizes within a sample is often very wide—for example, a cave sediment may contain pieces of rock with diameters millions of times those of the clay particles filling their interstices. An ordinary linear scale for particle size is therefore impractical, and a graduated or geometric scale is necessary. Many scales and grade classifications have been devised, a correlation between the most commonly used being shown in *Table 8.2*.

Udden's scale (Udden, 1898) was geometric, taking 1 mm as the starting point and using the ratios $\frac{1}{2}$ or 2, depending on the direction, to obtain grade limits. The resulting system was useful but non-cyclic and non-regular. The Udden scale was modified by Wentworth (1922), who refined and elaborated it. The Wentworth scale is not, however, suited to the analysis of well-sorted deposits, such as dune sand, since the grade limits are too wide. The classes may be divided into two sub-groups, but this produces irrational numbers which are difficult to memorise. For this reason the Tyler standard (Tyler, 1930) was developed, which had the mid-point of each class as a whole number or a fraction. The British Standard classification (British Standard 410:1969) has been widely used, but by far the best system is the ϕ (phi) scale of Krumbein (1934), to which reference has already been made. This is based on the fact that the class limits of the

Table 8.3 PHI (ϕ)–MILLIMETER CONVERSION TABLE

ϕ	$+\phi$ (mm)	$-\phi$ (mm)	ϕ	$+\phi$ (mm)	$-\phi$ (mm)
0	1.00	1.00	5.0	0.031	32.00
0.25	0.84	1.18	5.25	0.026	38.05
0.5	0.70	1.41	5.5	0.022	45.25
0.75	0.61	1.68	5.75	0.018	53.81
1.0	0.50	2.00	6.0	0.015	64.00
1.25	0.42	2.37	6.25	0.013	76.10
1.5	0.35	2.82	6.5	0.011	90.51
1.75	0.29	3.36	6.75	0.009	—
2.0	0.25	4.00	7.0	0.007	—
2.25	0.21	4.75	7.25	0.006	—
2.5	0.17	5.65	7.5	0.005	—
2.75	0.14	6.72	7.75	0.004	—
3.0	0.12	8.00	8.0	0.003	—
3.25	0.10	9.51	8.25	0.003	—
3.5	0.08	11.31	8.5	0.0028	—
3.75	0.07	13.45	8.75	0.0023	—
4.0	0.06	16.00	9.0	0.0020	—
4.25	0.05	19.02	9.25	0.0016	—
4.5	0.04	22.62	9.5	0.0014	—
4.75	0.037	26.90	9.75	0.0012	—

Udden scale can be expressed as powers of 2. Krumbein preferred to use the logarithm of the diameter (to the base 2) rather than the measured diameter, and to avoid negative numbers this logarithm was multiplied by -0. Thus $\phi = -\log_2$ diameter (mm).

The system is easily memorable and mathematically sound; its value is shown in the processing and interpretation of results (p. 105). It forms the basis of nearly all recent work on particle size, and has the additional advantage of being standardised. A correlation between the ϕ values and their metric equivalents is shown in *Table 8.3*, for $\frac{1}{2}\phi$ intervals.

PARTICLE SIZING

The flow chart (*Figure 8.2*) illustrates the processes which together compose a complete particle size analysis. Inexperienced analysts tend to progress directly from sample—analysis—evaluation of results, without a careful consideration of the theoretical background to their work. All the sub-stages (for example, sample splitting or pre-treatment) are just as important

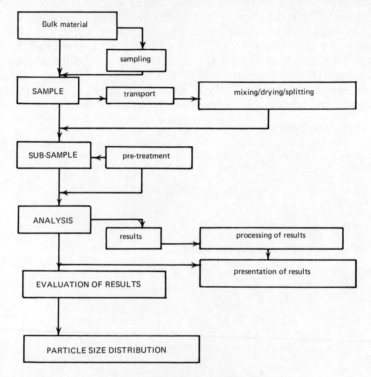

Fig. 8.2. Flow chart for particle size analysis

as the main analysis, and just as liable to produce inaccuracies. Numerous techniques to obtain a size distribution are available, and several useful comparative summaries have been published (Lapple, 1968; Hurst and Spence, 1969). The techniques vary greatly in complexity and in the amount of delicate and expensive apparatus required. Sophisticated methods such as the use of a gas laser or electronic particle counter are often impractical for archaeological work. There are, however, numerous laboratories and commercial firms who will undertake automated analyses on a contract basis. This is necessarily expensive but has the great advantage of being quick. Obtaining a particle size distribution is usually a slow process, although this obviously depends to some extent on the method chosen. If a large number of samples are to be processed in a short time, it may be worth while investing in the services provided by one of these laboratories rather than spending money on operators' time for preparation and processing. Men are often more expensive than machines. Whatever method is employed, it is necessary to understand the technique in order to evaluate the results and use them in the interpretation of the sediment. *Table 8.4* summarises some of the most commonly used

Table 8.4 TECHNIQUES FOR PARTICLE SIZE ANALYSIS

Technique	Suitable size range	Notes
Direct measurement	Boulders, pebbles and cobbles	See p. 42
Sieving (dry)		
vibratory	Pebbles and sand	See p. 111
airjet	Sand	See p. 114
Sieving (wet)		
flush	Fine sand/coarse silt	See p. 114
precision		
electroformed sieves	Fine sand/coarse silt	See p. 114
Microscopy		
light	Sand/silt	See p. 135
electron	Silt/clay	
automated	Sand/silt/clay	See p. 139
Electronic particle-counting	Sand/silt	See p. 143 (Coulter Counter)
Sedimentation		
elutriation	Silt/clays	See p. 146 (not a recommended method)
settling tubes	Sand/silt/clay	See p. 124 (Bottom withdrawal tube and Stairmand's tube)
pipette	Silt/clay	See p. 118 (Andreasen method)
hydrometer	Silt/clay	See p. 124
sedimentation balances	Silt/clay	See p. 130 (Bostock balance)
optical photoextinction	Silt/clay	See p. 131 (EEL photoextinction sedimentometer)
Centrifuge	Clay	See p. 147 (Disc centrifuge)
Air permeability	Sand/silt	See p. 146 (not recommended)

analytical techniques, together with an indication of their recommended work range and the 'size' measurement obtained. Operating procedures and further discussion may be found below (Chapters 9–12).

PRESENTATION AND INTERPRETATION OF PARTICLE SIZE ANALYSIS RESULTS

In order that the maximum amount of information may be obtained, the results of a particle size analysis must be presented in a suitable manner, ideally one which permits of direct inter-sample comparison. The raw data should be available in tabular form, as a number, a volume or a weight/size distribution, expressed in terms of ϕ units.

TABULAR PRESENTATION

Obviously, the simplest method of expressing data is to leave them in as a table, just as they were recorded on the work-sheet (*Figure 9.2*), or converted to percentages. However, this makes it impossible to visualise the size distribution and is no help at all when samples or sites are compared. The data table should be used as a necessary step in the final production of data in a graphical form, or in mathematical or statistical treatment.

HISTOGRAMS

The histogram or bar graph is used to show the percentage of grains in each size class. It has the advantage of being very simple to construct, but the great disadvantage of a lack of standardisation. The choice of class widths in the histogram is very important. With a narrowly divided sediment—for example, one sieved at $\frac{1}{4}$ or $\frac{1}{2}\phi$ intervals—an arithmetic distribution is acceptable, but it is more accurate to use a logarithmic scale. The shape of the histogram depends on the class intervals used, and *Figure 8.3* shows the appearance of two histograms constructed from the same set of data but using different class widths. The final appearance is quite different.

Two basic methods are available for the construction of a histogram:

(1) Construct a rectangle over each chosen class unit, the size of which is proportional to the number (or percentage) of particles in that unit.
(2) Construct a rectangle whose *area* is proportional to the number of particles in that unit. The total area under the histogram is therefore equal to the number of particles counted, ideally reduced to 100 by making the rectangles equal to the percentage of particles in the unit. Histograms made on this basis may be compared irrespective of the number of particles that were sized.

The histogram is not, however, recommended as a method of presentation, since it is impossible to make further statistical or mathematical deductions from it. The visual impact of the method is useful in some cases, particularly in detecting bimodality or polymodality in samples. *Figure 8.4* shows a histogram constructed from data obtained from a particle size analysis of a sediment stratified in a coastal Iron Age site at Hengistbury Head, Hants. The bimodal character of the sample is clear, a major mode occurring in the fine sand grade and a minor mode in fine silt/clay. The sediment was therefore likely to represent the product of two different depositional environments. The textural characteristics of the sample suggested that it was deposited under tidal estuarine conditions, the sand

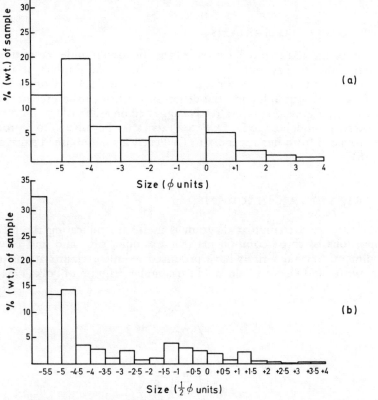

Fig. 8.3. Histograms of the same particle size distribution, expressed in (a) 1 φ units, and (b) ½ φ units

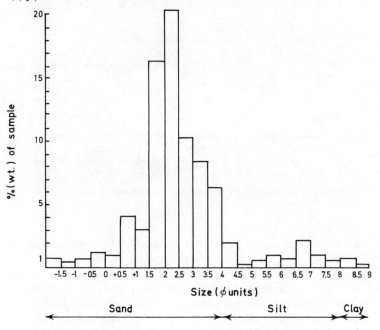

Fig. 8.4. Histogram of the particle size composition of a bimodal estuarine sandy deposit from Hengistbury Head, Hants.

fraction being of a markedly marine type, deposited under conditions of high available energy, and the finer mode being the product of a more tranquil depositional environment. The sample was taken from a critical point in the stratigraphy and the diagnosis confirmed the presence of an estuarine transgression phase already suggested on archaeological grounds. (The writer is indebted to Dr D. P. S. Peacock for permission to reproduce these remarks from her appendix to Dr Peacock's unpublished excavation report.)

TRIANGULAR DIAGRAMS

The format of a triangular diagram is useful for indicating the relative proportions of three components (for example, silt, sand and clay) in a sediment. Several writers have produced sediment classifications using such means, and *Figure 8.5* shows the triangular diagram of Folk (1954) for

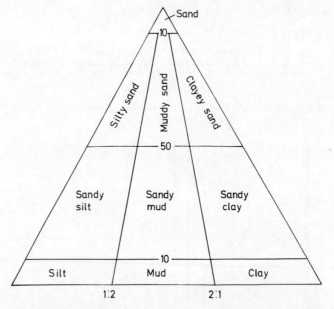

Fig. 8.5. Triangular diagram for expressing the composition of sediments (after Folk, 1954)

sand/silt/clay mixtures. The principle is exactly the same as that already described for the plotting of pebble shape data (p. 46). The diagrams are very simple to construct and may be useful in showing clusters and general trends if a large quantity of samples has been analysed. The method of Folk is a useful way of obtaining a standardised sediment description, and can be combined with calculated descriptive parameters (p. 101).

SEMI-PICTORIAL GRAPHS

The use of a semi-pictorial graph has long been a popular method for the presentation of obvious changes in particle size composition in a stratified series, since it is particularly suitable for the non-specialist or in cases where only the broad changes in composition are required. It may also be used where some sampling characteristic or other factor renders the use of more sophisticated methods unsuitable. The writer has pointed out the inadequacy of the form elsewhere (Shackley, 1972) and compared the potential of such diagrams with calculated statistics. The method is particularly suitable for the presentation of textural changes in cave sediments (Lais, 1941; Schmidt, 1958; Laville, 1970; Laville and de Sonneville-Bordes, 1967; Shackley, 1972, 1973a).

Figure 8.6 illustrates an example of such a graph, used to record textural changes obtained from particle size analysis of a series of cave deposits at

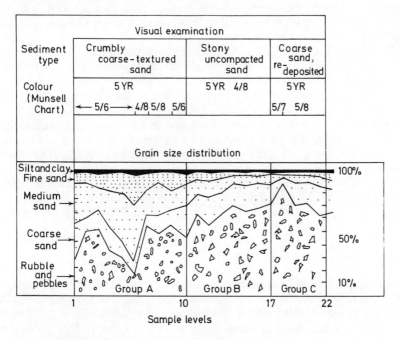

Fig. 8.6. Semi-pictorial graph for presenting the results of a particle size analysis on a sample series from the Badger Hole (Wookey, England). The analysis is combined with a visual description and a Munsell colour designation (after Shackley, 1972)

the Badger Hole (Wookey, Mendip Hills). The stratigraphic series was sampled at 10 cm intervals and the sample layers are plotted on the horizontal axis of the diagram. The cumulative percentage of each sample at $\frac{1}{2}\phi$ intervals from -6 to $+4\phi$ was calculated, and plotted on the appropriate vertical axes. The lines delimiting each unit were then joined, so that a picture of the changes in the amount of material in that class unit up the sediment column could be obtained. However, for the sake of simplicity the resulting complex of lines was simplified by showing only the major sediment type boundaries. Easy interpretation is facilitated by the adoption of a semi-pictorial approach—for example, by representing the different grades of sands as variously sized dots, or thermoclastic scree as a complex of angular particles. Any interpretation of depositional environment from such a diagram alone is extremely subjective, since the trend lines mask features such as bimodality, and there is little standardisation.

In this particular series three major sediment zones were apparent, on the basis of broad textural changes accompanied by changes in colour and included matter. These are marked on *Figure 8.6*. This hypothesis was then tested by the construction of cumulative frequency curves for each sample, and the calculation of the Inclusive Graphic Statistics of Folk and Ward (1957). It was found that the statistical procedures were in reasonable agreement with the semi-pictorial graph, but that several samples differed in detail from the general trend in ways that were obscured by the limitations of the method (Shackley, 1972).

It has long been realised that cave sediments may represent an accurate picture of climatic change, owing to the sensitive and controlled environment of deposition present in the cave. Changes in sediment composition may often be correlated with changes in fauna—for example, the occurrence of ptarmigan, arctic fox and lemming will usually coincide with a thermoclastic scree that has been produced in a cold environment, rather than a fine-grained deposit produced by chemical weathering of the cave walls under more temperate conditions (Shackley, 1973a). This basic hypothesis has been the foundation for much recent interdisciplinary work on cave sediments—for example, that by Campbell (1969), Laville (1970, 1975), Fedele (1975) and Tankard and Schweitzer (1975).

CUMULATIVE FREQUENCY CURVES

The construction of a cumulative frequency curve is the preferred method of presenting a particle size distribution, and consists of plotting the grain size grades used (ideally on the ϕ scale) against the cumulative percentage of the sample occurring in them. Early work was done with an arithmetic scale, which tended to produce S-shaped distributions. This is now considered inaccurate. Since the drawing of such a curve is a necessary preliminary to the calculation of graphic statistics, optimum accuracy is required. The use of arithmetic probability paper is essential for any truly quantitative work. Since virtually all natural sediments are log normal, the curve for a unimodal sediment is likely to approach a straight line, and it is far easier to see sample differences between straight lines than between markedly S-shaped curves.

After such a curve has been constructed for each analysis (*Figure 8.7*), it is possible to read off percentile values, to standardise size frequency distributions and to describe them accurately. If a series of curves is to be drawn and compared, then the semi-transparent variety of arithmetic probability paper is useful. If a set of analyses always seems to produce bends in the curves in the same places, it is worth while checking the accuracy of the sieves, or the other sizing method being employed, since

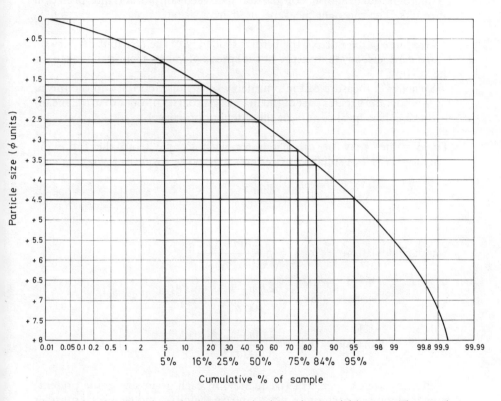

Fig. 8.7. A hypothetical particle size distribution curve plotted on arithmetic probability paper. The percentile values shown are for describing the curve by means of the Inclusive Graphic Statistics of Folk and Ward (1957)

this feature is more likely to be due to an experimental error than to some natural factor.

Percentile values are obtained by drawing a line from the required point on the horizontal (cumulative percentage) axis to intersect the curve, and another line at right angles from the intersection, to cut the vertical (ϕ unit) axis. The value is then read directly. Thus, in *Figure 8.7* the median grain diameter (50%) occurs at $+2.57\,\phi$. The use of arithmetic probability paper permits of accurate readings to $\pm 0.01\%$ (Folk and Ward, 1957), and expands the 'tails' of the size distribution.

STATISTICAL MEASURES

MOMENT STATISTICS

The calculation of moment statistics or measures for each particle size distribution enables it to be characterised by a set of numbers. This facilitates standardisation, comparisons between samples and interpretation of results. The moment measures used are:

  Mean size (a measure of the central tendency of the distribution curve)
  Standard deviation (a measure of the spread of values around the mean, or the 'sorting')
  Skewness (a measure of the symmetry of the distribution and the mean, i.e. whether the greater part of the material is coarser or finer than the mean)
  Kurtosis (the 'peakedness' of the distribution curve).

These values may be calculated for each sample from the following equations. A set of suitable procedures is given by Griffiths (1967).

$$\text{Mean} = \bar{x}_\phi = \frac{\Sigma fm}{n}$$

$$\text{Standard deviation} = \sigma_\phi = \sqrt{\left(\frac{\Sigma f(m - \bar{x}_\phi)^2}{100}\right)}$$

$$\text{Skewness} = \text{Sk}_\phi = \frac{\Sigma f(m - \bar{x}_\phi)^3}{100\, \sigma_\phi{}^3}$$

$$\text{Kurtosis} = \text{K}_\phi = \frac{\Sigma f(m - \bar{x}_\phi)^4}{100\sigma_\phi{}^4}$$

where f = weight per cent (frequency) in each grain size grade present; m = midpoint of each grain size grade (in ϕ units); and n = total number in sample (which is 100 when f is in percentage).

  Calculations are simplified if a computer program is used, although they can be done with a desk calculator (Kane and Hulbert, 1963; Schlee and Webster, 1967). Problems arise with 'open-ended' distributions, which may result if the pan fraction of a dry sieve analysis (the material finer than $4\,\phi$) is too large. Further subdivision is then required, usually by sedimentation, so that no more than 0.5% of the sample remains unsized (Folk, 1955; Griffiths, 1967).

GRAPHIC COMPUTATIONAL TECHNIQUES

These methods are used for describing the size frequency curve and accurately distinguishing different sediments, processes and environments.

Many different sets of parameters have been proposed, but the most commonly used are those of Inman (1962) and Folk and Ward (1957), which are summarised in *Table 8.5*. The first step in the calculation is to obtain a table of values, as in *Figure 9.2* (p. 111), and to plot a cumulative percentage frequency curve of the size distribution. The percentiles required for the particular set of statistics chosen are shown in *Table 8.5*,

Table 8.5 GRAPHIC STATISTICS

Measurement	Inman, 1962	Folk and Ward, 1957
Mean size	$M_\phi = \dfrac{(\phi 16 - \phi 84)}{2}$	$M_Z = \dfrac{(\phi 16 + \phi 50 + \phi 84)}{3}$
Standard deviation	$\dfrac{\phi 84 - \phi 16}{2}$	$\dfrac{\phi 84 - \phi 16}{4} + \dfrac{\phi 95 - \phi 5}{6.6}$
Skewness	$\alpha_{1\,\phi} = \dfrac{\phi 16 - \phi 84 - 2(\phi 50)}{\phi 84 - \phi 16}$	$Sk_{1\,\phi} = \dfrac{\phi 84 + \phi 16 - 2(\phi 50)}{2(\phi 84 - \phi 16)} + \dfrac{\phi 95 + \phi 5 - 2(\phi 50)}{2(\phi 95 - \phi 5)}$
Kurtosis	$\phi = \dfrac{(\phi 95 - \phi 5) - (\phi 84 - \phi 16)}{\phi 84 - \phi 16}$	$K_G = \dfrac{\phi 95 - \phi 5}{2.44(\phi 75 - \phi 25)}$

and may be read directly from the curve. The writer usually uses the Inclusive Graphic Statistics of Folk and Ward, which require the reading of the $5\,\phi$, $15\,\phi$, $25\,\phi$, $50\,\phi$, $75\,\phi$, $84\,\phi$ and $95\,\phi$ percentiles. Folk (1966) presented a comparison of the efficiency of the various statistics proposed by writers such as Trask (1930), Otto (1939), Inman (1952), Folk and Ward (1957), McCammon (1962) and Krumbein and Pettijohn (1938).

AUTOMATED DATA PROCESSING

Figure 8.8 shows the cumulative particle size distribution of a beach sand deposit stratified within a series of marine terrace gravels at Newport, Isle of Wight. Control samples of beach and dune sand from modern contexts are shown for comparison, and it can be seen that the cumulative curve brings out the distinction very clearly. These curves have been plotted from the data obtained from a dry sieve analysis (at $\frac{1}{2}\,\phi$ intervals), a computer program SIEVETTE being used to perform all the calculations and to describe the curves. The actual printout obtained from the analysis of the ancient beach sand is shown in *Figure 8.9*, obtained from the ICL 1900 computer at the University of Southampton. This program requires data input of the weights of sediment retained on each sieve, and will then calculate percentages and cumulative percentages. The percentile values are obtained by a linear extrapolation and the moment measures of the distribution are calculated, together with the Inclusive Graphic Statistics of Folk and Ward (1957) and the statistics of Inman (1962). The program also calculates the percentages of gravel, sand and 'mud' (silt and clay), and produces a textural description according to the criteria of Folk (1954). If the fine fraction is analysed by the pipette methods, the program will

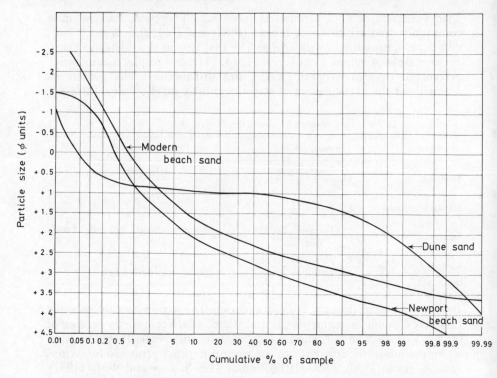

Fig. 8.8. Particle size distribution curves (arithmetic probability paper) for an ancient beach sand (Newport, Isle of Wight), a modern beach sand and a dune sand

accept the weights of sediment that were obtained by evaporating suspension samples taken at $\frac{1}{2}$ or 1ϕ intervals, according to the initial aliquot method of Creager and Sternberg (1963). A full size distribution will then be produced, and a great deal of time saved. The data obtained are standardised and it is easy to compare samples. If further processing is required, the program can be linked to further computer packages for any statistical manipulations, or to a computer graphic display which will draw the cumulative curve or any other required diagrams. This particular program was compiled in the University of Southampton by Dr D. Frederick, and modified by the writer, from Bork (1970), Kane and Hulbert (1963) and Pierce and Good (1966). Similar programs for the processing of particle size data are described by Schlee and Webster (1967) and Petersen, Hussey and Matelski (1969).

This type of automated data processing for particle size results has been highly recommended by the writer elsewhere (Shackley, 1973b), since it combines speed, accuracy and clarity of presentation. The SIEVETTE program requires the curve to be drawn by hand if necessary for visual purposes, although to a certain extent the curve is obsolete, since the graphic statistics can be obtained from linear extrapolation by the computer. However, it is difficult to detect bimodality or experimental errors without

PARTICLE SIZE ANALYSIS
NEWPORT SAND

PHI	WEIGHT	PERCENT	CUM. PERCENT
-1.000	0.500	0.181	0.181
-0.500	0.410	0.148	0.329
0.000	0.070	0.025	0.355
0.500	0.690	0.250	0.605
1.000	0.640	0.232	0.836
1.500	8.430	3.052	3.888
2.000	12.160	4.402	8.290
2.500	47.480	17.187	25.477
3.000	84.530	30.599	56.076
3.500	95.160	34.447	90.523
4.000	24.080	8.717	99.239

SIEVED WEIGHT = 274.150   SEDIMENTED WEIGHT = 0.000   TOTAL WEIGHT = 276.251

POINTS FOUND BY LINEAR EXTRAPOLATION
****

PERCENTILE	PHI VALUE
1.0	1.027
5.0	1.626
16.0	2.224
25.0	2.486
50.0	2.901
75.0	3.275
84.0	3.405
95.0	3.757

Fig. 8.9. Computer printout of the program SIEVETTE, for the ancient beach sand shown in Fig. 8.8 (continued overleaf)

SEDIMENT DESCRIPTION
****
****

GRAIN SIZE PARAMETERS
****

MEDIAN GRAIN DIAMETER = 2.901

PARAMETER	MOMENT MEASURES	FOLK	INMAN
*********	***************	****	*****

** DATA TOO OPEN ENDED FOR MOMENT MEASURE STATISTICS **

	FOLK	INMAN
MEAN	2.843	2.815
STANDARD DEVIATION	0.618	0.591
VARIANCE	0.382	0.349
SKEWNESS	0.000	- 0.145
		- 0.354
KURTOSIS	1.107	0.804

PERCENTAGES OF CONSTITUENTS
****

GRAVEL = 0.181 SAND = 99.059 MUD = 0.760

FOLKS TEXTURAL DESCRIPTION
****

SLIGHTLY GRAVELLY SAND

MODERATELY SORTED

MESOKURTIC

COARSE SKEWED

Fig. 8.9 (continued). Computer printout of the program SIEVETTE, for the ancient beach sand shown in Fig. 8.8

the curves being drawn, and they facilitate comparison. Folk (1955) emphasised the need for the drawing of the curve as an aid to full understanding of the distribution, by commenting that no anthropologist could adequately characterise Brigitte Bardot by four measurements.

GEOLOGICAL MEANING AND INTERPRETATION OF GRAPHIC STATISTICS

The mean size parameter reflects the average size of the sediment, and is influenced by the source of supply, the agent and the environment of deposition. The existence of gaps in the size distributions of natural sediments has long been noted, and Wentworth (1933) remarked on the absence of the $-1\,\phi$ grade and $-8\,\phi$ grade in a large number of samples. Udden (1914) found a gap of 3–4 ϕ in the sand fraction of aeolian sediments. However, Griffiths (1957) attributes the gaps to inefficient laboratory techniques. The role of the source material is fundamental in controlling the size distribution, especially the eventual value of the mean (Folk, 1962; Folk and Robels, 1964).

The distinction between various types of sands has often been made by reference to the standard deviation and skewness parameters. Several writers have devised verbal limits for the parameter measurements, the most useful being those of Folk and Ward (1957). Sediments consisting largely of fine sand are usually the best-sorted, and it therefore follows that wind-transported material shows this characteristic as well. Sorting becomes progressively worse for coarser or finer sediments, which Inman (1949) explains as a result of fluid dynamics, although Folk and Ward (1957) consider that it is the result of a polymodal source.

It is usual to plot the parameters or statistics obtained against one another on two-dimensional scatter diagrams, to diagnose the origin of the sediment and to locate general trends in series of analyses (Folk and Ward, 1957; Shackley, 1972). The commonly used method of drawing circles around likely groupings is very inaccurate, and should be replaced by properly calculated correlation coefficients for the scatter diagram being considered (Moroney, 1951). Plots of skewness against kurtosis are particularly useful, and Mason and Folk (1958) found that they could separate dune, beach and river sands by this means. Skewness and kurtosis values seem to be the result of the mixing of two normal populations in various proportions in the resulting sediments. Beach sands usually have negative skewness values, although dune and river sands tend to be positively skewed. Kurtosis values tend to be high in lagoonal silts but low in beach sands, since the latter are more efficiently sorted. It has been suggested that the parameter values depend to a considerable extent on the amount of coarse material present, which tends to weight the distribution on one side. Fuller (1962) noted that the 2 ϕ size is often missing from sediments deposited in shallow water environments. Friedman (1961), in discussing the negative skewness of beach sands, concluded, after an analysis of over 250 samples, that it was a function of two forces of irregular strength which operate in different directions in a beach environment, namely the oncoming waves and the backwash. The former agent deposits the material, whereas the latter tends to remove the fine fraction, which results in the negative skewness. The relationship between the current required to move particles of different sizes has been discussed by Allen (1970) and Inman (1949).

Numerous papers have been written concerning the interpretation of grain size distributions. Palaeoclimatic changes expressed by changes in the particle size composition of cave sediments in archaeological contexts have been the subject of recent work by Laville (1970), Tankard and Schweitzer (1975), and Shackley (1972, 1973a). Dakaris *et al.* (1964) discussed the particle size distribution of sediment layers in various Greek cave sites obtained by wet sieving and hydrometer analysis—for example, the cave of Kokkinopolis. The particle size distribution curves showed that the samples examined were principally composed of clay, although they were at first thought to have been loessic in origin. Davidson (1973) studied the evolution of the tell site at Sitagroi by carrying out a particle size analysis and measurements of total phosphate content (p. 69), and the writer has worked on the environment of deposition of various fluviatile and marine deposits occurring in archaeological contexts (p. 105). Cornwall (1959) described a combination of particle size analysis and chemical tests on soil samples from the ditch section of the Nutbane long barrow in Hampshire, and Smith and Simpson (1966) consider a similar set of problems posed during the excavation of a round barrow at Overton Hill, North Wiltshire. At the cave site of Asprochaliko (Higgs and Vita-Finzi, 1966) a granulometric analysis was carried out by dry sieving, note also being taken of colour changes and the declination of stones at the base of the deposit. Campbell (1969) made climatic reconstructions from similar work on several British Upper Palaeolithic cave sites, correlating changes with floral changes visible in pollen diagrams. Fedele (1975) has carried out similar work in the Italian Alps. The writer discusses the identification of estuarine sediments (p. 94), the distinction between blown and waterlain silt (p. 145) and the development of a buried soil profile (p. 85) from grain size distributions elsewhere in this volume.

Geological papers on the interpretation of grain size distributions include Fuller (1962) and Mason and Folk (1958).

The particle size distribution of a sediment should be used as the best way of quantifying and describing it, and as an objective method for comparing individual samples, stratigraphic series and different sites. It is also possible to diagnose the environment of deposition from particle size distributions, and to make observations concerning diagenetic factors. The results obtained from particle size analysis should be combined with chemical tests or micromorphological studies for a full characterisation.

References

ALLEN, J. R. L. (1970). *Physical Processes of Sedimentation Particle Analysis* (Halsted Press, Allen and Unwin, London)

ALLEN, T. (1968). *Particle Size Analysis* (Halsted Press, London)

BORK, K. B. (1970). 'Use of textural parameters in evaluating the genesis of the Berne Conglomerate', *Journal of Sedimentary Petrology*, **40** (3), 1007–1017

British Standard 410: 1969. 'Test sieves'

CAMPBELL, J. B. (1969). 'Excavations at Cresswell Crags', *Derbyshire Archaeological Journal*, **89**, 48–58

CHAYES, F. (1949). 'A simple point counter for thin section analysis', *American Mineralogist*, **34**, 1–11

CORNWALL, I. W. (1959). 'Report on the soil samples from the ditch section at Nutbane', *Proceedings of the Prehistoric Society*, **25**, 15–52

CREAGER, J. S. and STERNBERG, R. W. (1963). 'Comparative evaluation of three techniques of pipette analysis', *Journal of Sedimentary Petrology*, **33**, 462–466

DAKARIS, S. I., HIGGS, E. S. and HEY, R. W. (1964). 'Climate, environment and industries of Stone Age Greece', *Proceedings of the Prehistoric Society*, **30**, 199–245

DAVIDSON, D. A. (1973). 'Particle size and phosphate analysis—evidence for the evolution of a tell', *Archaeometry*, **15** (1), 143–152

FEDELE, F. (1975). 'Sediments as paleo-land segments', in *Geoarchaeology: Earth Science and the Past*, ed. Davidson, D. A. and Shackley, M. L. (Duckworth, London)

FERET, L. R. (1931). 'La grosseur des grains des matières pulvérulentes', *Assoc. Internat. pour l'Essai des Mat.*, Vol 2D, Zurich

FOLK, R. L. (1954). 'The distinction between grain size and mineral composition in sedimentary rock nomenclature', *Journal of Geology*, **62**, 334–359

FOLK, R. L. (1955). 'Student operator error in determination of roundness, sphericity and grain size', *Journal of Sedimentary Petrology*, **25**, 297–301

FOLK, R. L. (1962). 'Of skewness and sands', *Journal of Sedimentary Petrology*, **32**, 1451–1461

FOLK, R. L. (1966). 'A review of grain size parameters', *Sedimentology*, **6**, 73–93

FOLK, R. L. and ROBLES, R. (1964). 'Carbonate sediments of Isla, Perez, Alacran reef complex, Yucatan', *Journal of Geology*, **72**, 255–292

FOLK, R. L. and WARD, W. C. (1957). 'Brazos River bar, a study in the significance of grain size parameters', *Journal of Sedimentary Petrology*, **27**, 3–27

FRIEDMAN, G. M. (1961). 'Distinction between dune, beach and river sands from their textural characteristics', *Journal of Sedimentary Petrology*, **28**, 151–163

FRIEDMAN, G. M. (1962). 'Comparison of moment measures for sieving and thin section data in sedimentary petrological studies', *Journal of Sedimentary Petrology*, **32**, 15–25

FULLER, A. O. (1962). 'Systematic fractionation of sand in the shallow marine and beach environment off the South African coast', *Journal of Sedimentary Petrology*, **31**, 256–261

GRIFFITHS, J. C. (1967). *Scientific Method in Analysis of Sediments* (McGraw-Hill, New York)

HEYWOOD, H. (1947). *Symposium on Particle Size Analysis*, Institute of Chemical Engineers, 114

HIGGS, E. F. and VITA-FINZI, C. (1966). 'The climate, environment and industries of Stone Age Greece. Part II', *Proceedings of the Prehistoric Society*, **32**, 1–30

HURST, W. and SPENCE, G. (1969). 'The standardization of the particle size of abrasives', *Journal of the British Ceramic Society*, **6** (3), 60–65

INMAN, D. L. (1949). 'Sorting of sediments in the light of fluid mechanics', *Journal of Sedimentary Petrology*, **19**, 51–70

INMAN, D. L. (1962). 'Measures for describing the size distributions of sediments', *Journal of Sedimentary Petrology*, **22**, 125–145

KANE, W. T. and HULBERT, J. F. (1963). 'Fortran program for the calculation of grain size textural parameters on the IBM 1620 computer', *Sedimentology*, **2**, 87–90

KRUMBEIN, W. C. (1934). 'Size frequency distribution of sediments', *Journal of Sedimentary Petrology*, **4**, 65–77

KRUMBEIN, W. C. (1935). 'Thin section mechanical analysis of indurated sediments', *Journal of Geology*, **43**, 482–496

KRUMBEIN, W. C. and PETTIJOHN, F. J. (1938). *Manual of Sedimentary Petrography* (Appleton, New York)

LAIS, R (1941). 'Über Hohlensedimente', *Quartar*, **3**, 567

LAPPLE, C. E. (1968). 'Particle size analysis and analyzers', *Chemical Engineering*, **75** (11), 149–156

LAVILLE, H. (1970). 'L'abri magdalenien du Flageolet II', *Bulletin de la Societe prehistorique française*, **67**, 475–488

LAVILLE, H. (1975). 'The fill of rock shelters; methods of analysis and climatic interpretation', in

Geoarchaeology: Earth Science and the Past, ed. Davidson, D. A. and Shackley, M. L. (Duckworth, London)

LAVILLE, H. and DE SONNEVILLE-BORDES, D. (1967). 'Sedimentologie des niveaux mousteriens et aurignaciens de Caminade—Est', *Bulletin de la Societe prehistorique française*, **64**, 35–52

LITTLEJOHN, R. F. (1970). 'Particle size analysis', *Bulletin of the British Coal Util. Res. Assn*, **34** (5), 120–126

MCCAMMON, R. B. (1962). 'Efficiencies of percentile measures for describing the mean size and sorting of sedimentary particles', *Journal of Geology*, **70**, 453–465

MARTIN, G. (1926). 'Researches on the theory of fine grinding', *Transactions of the Ceramic Society*, **23**, 61

MASON, C. C. and FOLK, R. L. (1958). 'Differentiation of beach, dune and aeolian flat environments by size analysis', *Journal of Sedimentary Petrology*, **28**, 211–226

MORONEY, M. (1951). *Facts from Figures* (Penguin, Harmondsworth)

OTTO, G. H. (1939). 'A modified logarithmic probability graph for the interpretation of mechanical analysis of sediments', *Journal of Sedimentary Petrology*, **9**, 62–76

PETERSEN, G. W., HUSSEY, G. A. and MATELSKI, R. P. (1969). 'Processing and plotting of laboratory particle size data by digital computer', *Soil Science*, **108**, 448–449

PIERCE, J. W. and GOOD, D. I. (1966). 'Fortran II program for standard-size analysis of unconsolidated sediments using an IBM 1620 computer', Special distribution paper 28, State Geological Survey, Univ. of Kansas, USA

PIETSCH, W. (1968). 'An evaluation of techniques for particle size analysis', *Minerals Processing*, **6**, 11

ROSEN, H. N. and HULBERT, H. M. (1970). 'Size analysis of irregularly shaped particles in sieving: comparison with the Coulter Counter,' *Industrial and Engineering Chemistry—Fundamentals*, **9** (4), 658–661

SCHLEE, J. and WEBSTER, J. (1967). 'A computer program for grain size data', *Sedimentology*, **8** (1), 45–53

SCHMIDT, E. (1958). *Hohlenforschung und sedimentanalyse Schriften d. Inst. f. Ur-u. Fruh geschte der Schweiz*, No. 13

SHACKLEY, M. L. (1972). 'The use of textural parameters in the analysis of cave sediments', *Archaeometry*, **14** (1), 133–145

SHACKLEY, M. L. (1973a). 'Computers and sediment analysis in archaeology', *Science in Archaeology*, **9**, 29–30

SHACKLEY, M. L. (1973b). 'The Alveston Bone Fissure' (with H. Taylor), *Proceedings of the Univ. of Bristol Speleological Society*, **13** (2), 135–152

SMITH, I. F. and SIMPSON, D. D. A. (1966). 'Excavation of a round barrow on Overton Hill, North Wiltshire, England', *Proceedings of the Prehistoric Society*, **32**, 122–156

TANKARD, A. J. and SCHWEITZER, F. (1975). 'Textural analysis of cave sediments: Die Kelders, Cape Province, South Africa', in *Geoarchaeology: Earth Science and the Past*, ed. Davidson, D. A. and Shackley, M. L. (Duckworth, London)

TRASK, P. D. (1930). 'Mechanical analysis of sediments by centrifuge', *Economic Geology*, **25**, 581–599

TYLER, W. S. (1930). *The Profitable Use of Testing Sieves*, Clevely, Ohio (company publication)

UDDEN, J. A. (1898). *Mechanical Composition of Wind Deposits*, Augustana Library publication No. 1

UDDEN, J. A. (1914). 'Mechanical composition of clastic sediments', *Bull. Geol. Soc. America*, **25**, 655–744

VAN DER PLAS, L. (1962). 'Preliminary note on the granulometric analysis of sedimentary rocks', *Sedimentology*, **1**, 145–157

WADELL, H. A. (1935). 'Volume, shape and roundness of quartz particles', *Journal of Geology*, **43**, 250–280

WENTWORTH, C. K. (1922). 'The shapes of pebbles', *Bull. U.S. Geol. Survey*, **730-C**, 91–114

WENTWORTH, C. K. (1933). 'The shape of rock particles: a discussion', *Journal of Geology*, **41**, 306–309

Chapter 9

PARTICLE SIZE ANALYSIS BY SIEVING

SIEVE TYPES

Sieving is the easiest and most popular means of size analysis, and for this reason is also the one most liable to error. It is not just a matter of pouring some sample into one end of a sieve column, shaking it and recording the weights retained on each sieve. A properly planned dry sieving operation is, however, the best way of obtaining a size distribution for particles of diameters 63 μm–100 mm ($+4\,\phi$ to $-6\,\phi$). There are numerous varieties of sieves, the most commonly used being the American ASTM series (American Society for Testing Materials, 1966), the Tyler series (Tyler, 1930) and the British Standard Sieves (BS 410, 1969)[2]. Each series consists of a set of sieves of different mesh apertures. For the coarser sieves the mesh is usually constructed of woven brass or mild steel, phosphor bronze being used for the finer sieves (mesh widths less than 250 μm, $2\,\phi$), and electro-formed nickel mesh for micromesh sieves. Sieves are available in different sizes (3, 4, 8 and 12 in diameters), the 8 in variety being the most commonly used. The larger size is useful for site work, particularly the extraction of molluscan or seed/grain remains. Sieves for size analysis are best spaced at either 0.5 ϕ or 0.25 ϕ intervals.

CARE AND TESTING OF SIEVES

All sieves are precision instruments and must be treated with great care. The same set should never be used for wet and dry sieving, and the temptation to dry sieve meshes in an oven should be resisted. After the completion of an analysis the sieve should be cleaned by gentle brushing, a brass wire brush being used for meshes coarser than 2.5 ϕ and a nylon brush for fine meshes. Since the sieve mesh is woven like a fabric and not welded in any way, the use of spatulas or screwdrivers to dislodge persistent particles is to be condemned. A graphic illustration of the kind of damage that can be done is shown in *Figure 9.1*.

The manufacturer usually runs stringent tests on sieve meshes in the

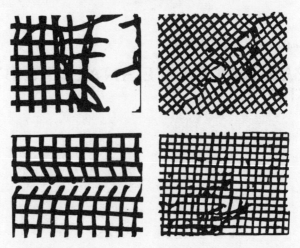

Fig. 9.1. Damage to sieve meshes due to bad cleaning (after Pietsch, 1968)

laboratory, but a standard sample of suitably calibrated glass beads may be used to check mesh apertures, a wise precaution if a very large number of analyses is to be run. Mesh accuracy may also be checked by placing the sieve under a microscope and measuring a section of the mesh with a micrometer eyepiece (Ingram, 1971). Periodic checks are to be recommended. Placing too great a weight on a sieve will ruin the mesh and make the analytical results very inaccurate (Pietsch, 1968). *Table 9.1* presents the recommended maximum load for various sieve meshes, in a set spaced at 0.5 ϕ intervals, but this will vary slightly if different spacings are used (McManus, 1965; Shergold, 1946).

Sieving time is another crucial factor. Most workers now agree that a

Table 9.1 MAXIMUM PERMISSIBLE LOAD ON 8 in DIAMETER SIEVES
(after Ingram, 1971)

Sieve mesh size ϕ value		Maximum weight (g)
−2	4.70 mm	80
−1.5	2.82	68
−1	2.00	56
−0.5	1.41	48
0	1.00	40
+0.5	700 μm	34
1	500	28
1.5	352	24
2	251	20
2.5	178	17
3	124	15
3.5	88	12
4	62	10
4.5	44	8
5	31	7

sieving time of 10 min per nest in vibratory dry sieving is adequate, although some still believe 15 min to be essential. Kaye (1962) and Whitby (1958) suggest theoretical end-points to a sieving operation.

The size distribution obtained from a sieve analysis is therefore a function of the degree of wear on the sieves, the load put upon them, the duration of the sieving operation and any sampling errors, as well as variations in the sieve apertures or errors due to carelessness or different operators. All these points should be borne in mind when the results of the analysis are being interpreted.

DRY SIEVE ANALYSIS (vibration method)

The following method is suitable for the dry sieve analysis of material in the approximate size range $-6\,\phi$ to $+4\,\phi$.

Site Badger Hole, Wookey		Sample No. B4/19/71	Exact Location. See drawing		
Pre-treatment Removal of Fe.++, wash dry, mix and riffle		Analyst MLS	Date 5.3.71.		
General description coarse clastic particles, some fine sand.		Notes Several Teeth and small bones removed.			
ϕ value	Sieve weight (g.)	Total weight (g.)	Sediment weight (g.)	Sediment % age	Cumulative % age
-6	501.10	501·01	–	–	–
-5.5	500.35	500·35	–	–	–
-5	545.38	583·16	37.78	16·74	16·74
-4.5	565.82	611·35	45.53	20·09	36·83
-4	566.56	615·44	48·88	21·66	58·50
-3.5	532.45	556·84	24.39	10·81	69·31
-3	531.74	546·43	14·69	6·51	75·82
-2.5	513.16	528·38	15.22	6·74	82·56
-2	494.34	502·57	8·23	3·64	86·21
-1.5	465.48	473·28	7·80	3·45	89·67
-1	472.12	477·65	5·53	2·36	92·18
-0.5	454.27	454·81	0·54	0·15	92·18
0	437.46	440·66	3·20	1·41	93·60
+0.5	415.84	418·46	2·62	1·16	94·76
+1	401.10	403·34	2·24	0·99	95·75
1.5	365.77	368·49	2·72	1·20	96·96
2	361.72	362·60	0·88	0·37	97·34
2.5	357.33	358·20	0·87	0·38	97·72
3	350.03	351·32	1·29	0·57	98·29
3.5	351.33	352·36	1·03	0·45	98·75
4	339.67	340·52	0·85	0·37	99·13
Pan 1	–	–	–	–	–
Pan 2	–	–			
Pan 3	339.20	340·52	1·32	0·69	99·82

(% age finer than 4ϕ)

Fig. 9.2. Record sheet for a dry sieve analysis. The example taken is from Layer 19, Badger Hole series (Fig. 8.6)

(1) Arrange a series of ASTM E11–61 8 in sieves in mesh size order, spacing them at $\frac{1}{2}\phi$ intervals from -6ϕ to $+4\phi$. Twenty-one sieves will be required, together with the appropriate lids and pans.

(2) Weigh each sieve on an accurate laboratory balance[19]. An electronic balance is preferable for speed and accuracy. Sieve weights should be recorded to three decimal places. Ensure that the sieves are perfectly clean and that the balance is periodically zeroed during the operation, if necessary. Since these weights will remain constant for a particular series, they may be printed on to the standard sieve analysis record sheet (*Figure 9.2*), but should be checked occasionally for variations due to wear.

(3) Dry and prepare the sample by any of the methods described in Chapter 3, and ensure that the sample size is sufficient for accurate analysis (p. 24). Very coarse material is not suitable for sieving and should be sized directly by a suitable hand method (p. 42). Record any pre-treatment of the sample, with subsequent weight changes, on the original sample record form (*Figure 4.1*, p. 34).

(4) Divide the whole series of sieves into a number of 'nests', since the vibratory shaker will not be able to cope with the whole series at once. Ensure that each 'nest' has a weighed pan at the bottom.

(5) Plug in the shaker and check that the lead is not tangled. The model shown in *Figure 9.3* is the Pascall 'Inclyno' test sieve shaker[18], which the writer has found to be efficient and reasonably quiet.

(6) Position the coarsest nest of sieves on the shaker, in descending mesh size order. Add the sample and clamp the sieve lid down very firmly. Set the timer for 10 or 15 min, after which time it should switch off automatically. It is useless to try and conduct other experiments such as sedimentation analysis or anything involving the use of a microscope while a vibratory shaker is in operation in the vicinity, since most peculiar effects will be obtained.

(7) After the shaker has switched itself off, remove the nest of sieves on to the bench and transfer the material in the pan into the top of the next nest. Repeat stages (6) and (7) until the sample has passed through all the sieves.

(8) Weigh the sieves with their load of sediment on an electronic balance, recording weights to three decimal places on the appropriate column of the record sheet (*Figure 9.2*).

(9) Brush the sieve carefully, tipping the sediment out into a plastics bag. Label and store. Store the fine fraction, which passed the 63 μm (4ϕ) sieve in an airtight sample phial, in case further subdivision by a sedimentation method is required.

After calculating the weight of sediment retained on each sieve, and converting this to percentages, you may find more than 0.5% of the sample is finer than 4ϕ. If this is so, then a sedimentation analysis will be required to ensure the statistical accuracy of the size distribution. The use of a simple computer program for these rather tedious calculations is strongly recommended, the SIEVETTE program described above (p. 101) being especially suitable. Sieving results should be reproducible to within $\pm$ 1%, if the sample has been properly taken, split and prepared. Occasional accuracy checks on sieve meshes reduce errors due to wear or bad cleaning. Results may then be presented by any of the methods described above (p. 96).

Figure 9.2 illustrates a suitable standard record sheet, with the results obtained from a dry sieve analysis of a cave sediment sample, taken from a

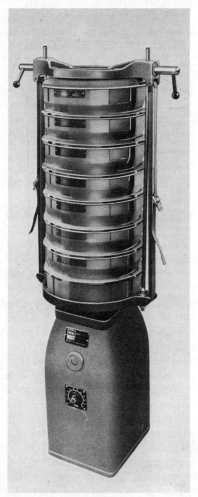

Fig. 9.3. The Pascall 'Inclyno' test-sieve shaker. (Reproduced by courtesy of the Pascall Engineering Co. Ltd)

stratigraphic series at the Badger Hole (Wookey, Mendip Hills). This sample can be seen to be rather coarse-grained, and the particles were extremely angular. The deposit represented was a thermoclastic scree produced by frost-shattering under very cold conditions, a conclusion which contributed to the pattern of palaeoenvironmental change built up from a study of the whole sequence (Shackley, 1972).

AIRJET SIEVING

The 'Alpine' airjet sieving method (Malhotra, 1967) represents an alternative to vibratory dry sieving, but has been little used. The general
principle involves the use of an air current to disperse the material on the
sieve and to carry the finer fraction through the mesh. The sediment is
lifted by the airjet, which clears the mesh and separates the particles, which
are gently drawn through the mesh by the return current. Only one sieve
may be used at a time, and the initial sample weight must not exceed 50 g.
The sample is processed for 6 min at a time, and at present the material
which has passed through the sieve is not recoverable with the standard
apparatus. The results are held to be more consistent than those obtained by
the vibration method, but the practical difficulties render the method unsuitable for archaeological work. A test machine built by W. Wahler uses
the same principle and processes a series of sieves at one time, but it is not
fully mechanised (Müller, 1967).

WET SIEVING

This technique may be used for sediments that will aggregate when dry
sieved. British Standard No. 1796 (1952) describes the available methods,
using conventional sieve meshes down to 44 μm. The same set of sieves
should never be used for both wet and dry sieving. Irani (1965) has
developed a semi-automatic apparatus for wet sieving using meshes of
5–50 μm, which can be extended to a wider 2–250 μm range. In the
apparatus of Longhurst and Bergstrom (1971) a standard sieve is mounted
on a drain pan on top of a vibrator. Water is added from a shower head
mounted on the sieve cover, the vibrator is activated and the undersized
particles are washed through.

Applications of these methods have been made by West and Dumbleton
(1972), who describe a process for washing a sample free of silt and clay and
then wet sieving the remaining fraction in a single operation. This is not,
however, suitable for very fine-grained sediments with little sand or gravel.
In an analysis of limestone Rexroad (1972) considered that wet sieving
gave better and more accurate results than dry methods, but this is not
generally true for unconsolidated sediments.

For archaeological purposes it is better to use wet sieving techniques only
for the removal of the fine fraction, and complete the analysis by vibratory
dry sieving of the coarser material and some form of sedimentation
analysis for the finer. The practical difficulties and the annoyance of having
to dry samples before weighing outweigh any possible advantage due to
less sample aggregation.

PRECISION ELECTROFORMED SIEVES

A technique that has recently become fashionable is the use of precision
electroformed sieves, sometimes in an ultrasonic bath, for accurate analysis

of very fine particles (Olaver, 1969). Daeschner (1969) recommends a method suitable for extremely agglomerated material in the size range 16–150 µm. The sieves used are the 3 in diameter ASTM E161–8 series[2], mounted on a special apparatus within a specimen funnel in a flask. While the sample is being washed through, pulses of positive suction are applied to the filter flask, which creates a 'breathing' action on each sieve plate. The entire process, using five or six sieves, takes about an hour, initial sample sizes of only 1–2 g being required. The size range and small sample size make the method attractive for archaeological purposes, but the high cost of the small precision sieves counts against it. Nucholls and Fuller (1965) used electroformed sieves in an ultrasonic bath to separate dust particles, but this method has numerous disadvantages. The ultrasonic wet sieving method is thought to be less efficient than ordinary vibratory dry sieving (Hall and Beddows, 1969), but may be useful if very small quantities of sandy material have to be analysed. The purchase of a set of small precision sieves for use in any of these series of apparatus cannot usually be justified for archaeological purposes alone.

References

ASTM E–11 (1968). 'Wire-cloth sieves for testing purposes', *1968 Book of ASTM Standards*, Vol. **30**, 107–112 (American Society for Testing Materials)

British Standard 410: 1969. 'Test sieves'

British Standard 1796: 1952. 'Methods for the use of British Standard fine-mesh test sieves'

DAESCHNER, H. W. (1969). 'Wet sieving with precision electroformed sieves', *Powder Technology*, **2** (6), 349–355

HALL, W. S. and BEDDOWS, J. K. (1969). 'Ultrasonic vibration on sieves', *Ultrasonics*, **7** (2)

INGRAM, R. L. (1971). 'Sieve analysis', in *Procedures in Sedimentary Petrology*, ed. Carver, R. (Wiley, New York)

IRANI, R. R. (1965). 'Particle size analysis with micromesh sieves', *International Journal of Powder Metallurgy*, **1** (4), 22–27

KAYE, B. H. (1962). Unpublished Ph.D. Thesis, University of London

LONGHURST, D. and BERGSTROM, B. H. (1971). 'Rapid method for dry sieve analysis to 500 mesh', *Minerals Processing*, **12** (4), 15

MCMANUS, D. A. (1965). 'A study of maximum load for small diameter screens', *Journal of Sedimentary Petrology*, **36**, 782–786

MALHOTRA, V. M. (1967). 'The Alpine airjet sieve: a new method for determining the fineness of cement', *Indian Concrete Journal*, **41** (8), 305–309

MÜLLER, G. (1967). *Methods in Sedimentary Petrology* (Hafner, Stuttgart)

NUCHOLLS, M. J. and FULLER, R. K. (1965). 'Sieve analysis of particles smaller than 44 µm in diameter', *Soil Science*, **10** (5), 292–295

OLAVER, O. (1969). 'The use of precision microsieves for particle size analysis', *Staub*, **20**, 69–71

PIETSCH, W. B. (1968). 'Evaluation of techniques for particle size analysis': Part 1, *Minerals Processing*, **9** (11), 6–11; Part 2, *Minerals Processing*, **9** (12), 12–14

REXROAD, P. R. (1972). 'Wet sieve analysis of limestone', *Journal of the Association of Analytical Chemists*, **55** (3), 539–541

SHACKLEY, M. L. (1972). 'The use of textural parameters in the analysis of cave sediments,' *Archaeometry*, **14** (1), 133–145

SHERGOLD, F. A. (1946). 'The effects of sieve loading on the results of sieve analysis of natural sands', *Soc. Chemical Industry Transactions*, **65**, 245–249

TYLER, W. S. (1930). *The Profitable Use of Testing Sieves* (company publication, Clevely, Ohio)

WEST, G. and DUMBLETON, M. J. (1972). *Wet Sieving for the Particle Size Distribution of Soils*, Transport and Road Research Lab. Report LR437

WHITBY, K. T. (1958). 'The mechanics of fine sievings', *ASTM Special Publication* **234** (3), 3–23

Chapter 10

PARTICLE SIZE ANALYSIS OF SEDIMENT SUSPENSIONS

THEORY

The particle size analysis of sediments dispersed in a liquid, usually water, is referred to as 'sedimentation'. Sedimentation analyses are used for fine material in the sub-sieve range, especially for subdivision of silts. It is usual to combine dry sieving with sedimentation to get a full size distribution. All the available sedimentation methods depend on Stokes's Law, which governs the frictional resistance of a fluid to a particle falling through it. Stokes's Law states that:

$$V = \frac{2gr^2(D_1 - D_2)}{9\eta} \tag{10.1}$$

where V = particle velocity; g = gravity acceleration; D_1 = density of the falling sphere; D_2 = density of the sedimentation liquid or gas; η = viscosity of the liquid; and r = radius of the sphere in cm. For a particle size analysis it is the particle radius (r) which is required. This may be calculated from Eq. 10.1 by use of Stokes's Law:

$$r = \sqrt{\left[\frac{9\eta}{2 \times g(D_1 - D_2)}\right]} \times \sqrt{\left(\frac{h}{t}\right)}(cm) \tag{10.2}$$

since $V = h/t$, where h = falling height (cm) and t = falling time (s). This enables the time required for a sphere of given size and density to fall through a given height in a given medium to be calculated. A further discussion of Stokes's Law may be found in Kösters (1960). Stokes's Law strictly only applies to particles finer than 4.5 ϕ. If this grain diameter is exceeded, then the formula of Oseen (Müller, 1967) must be applied, which states that:

$$V = \frac{A}{2r} + \sqrt{\left[\left(\frac{A}{r}\right)^2 + 4rB\right]} \tag{10.3}$$

116

where $A = 8\eta/3D_2$ and

$$B = \frac{16(D_1 - D_2) \times 9}{27D_2} \qquad (10.4)$$

Stokes's Law refers to spherical particles, but mineral grains are seldom, if ever, completely spherical. The 'size' being measured is therefore the Stokes diameter (p. 88), or the diameter of a particle which falls the same distance as a mineral sphere in the same time, through the same medium, at the same velocity (Müller, 1967). The diameter of the sphere forms the basis for the calculation of the settling velocity in the sedimentation apparatus. Thus, if the variables are known, the settling velocity, and therefore the particle size, may be calculated for any suspension of sediment. A slight problem arises if the sediment is polymineralic, since the density (D_1) chosen must be that of the predominant particle type. It is usual to take a value of 2.65, since the majority of sediments are composed chiefly of quartz. The particle concentration must not be less than 1% or too high, since this causes particles to interfere with each other during settling. A maximum weight of 10–25 g of sample per 1000 ml of fluid is recommended for pipette or hydrometer sedimentation, although lower concentrations will often give more accurate results (Irani and Callis, 1963).

The density and viscosity of the sedimentation fluid will vary with temperature. *Tables 10.1* and *10.2* list the values for the density and viscosity

Table 10.1   DENSITY AND VISCOSITY OF WATER

Temperature (°C)	Density	Viscosity
15	0.991 30	1.140
16	0.998 97	1.111
17	0.998 80	1.083
18	0.998 62	1.059
19	0.998 43	1.030
20	0.998 23	1.005
21	0.998 08	0.981
22	0.997 80	0.958
23	0.997 56	0.936
24	0.997 32	0.914
25	0.997 07	0.894

of water and for the density of minerals at various temperatures. The experimental temperature should be controlled by keeping the sedimentation cylinder (for pipette and hydrometer analysis) in a constant-temperature water-bath. At 20 °C the density and viscosity of water can be taken as 1. Atmospheric pressure is assumed and gravity acceleration conventionally taken as 980 g/cm³. This simplifies the Stokes equation to

$$r = \sqrt{\left[\frac{9}{2 \times g(2.65 - 1)}\right]} \times \sqrt{\left(\frac{r}{t}\right)} \qquad (10.5)$$

for quartz particles in water at 20 °C. The settling times of particles at fixed temperatures and fall heights must then be looked up in *Table 10.3*. Additional values can be calculated from Eq. 10.1. The particle size distribution of any sediment suspension can now be calculated from samples withdrawn at separate time–intervals. All the sedimentation methods make use of these basic principles, although the experimental methods and

Table 10.2 MINERAL DENSITIES

Mineral	Density
Quartz	2.65
Calcite	2.72
Dolorite	2.87
Mica	2.7–3.2
Muscovite	2.83
Chlorites	2.66 – > 3
Potash feldspars	2.57
Kaolinite	2.58
Albite	2.61
Anorthite	2.76

instruments used vary. The calculations for any particular method are less fearsome than might be supposed, since standardised sets of procedures are available, which can easily be performed with a desk calculator or computer. The results of sedimentation analyses may then be added to the size distributions obtained for the coarse fraction of the sample, and the final particle size distribution curve drawn (p. 102).

SEDIMENTATION USING THE PIPETTE METHOD

The analysis of suspended sediments by use of the Andreasen pipette is by far the most frequently used method, and is especially suitable for the fraction between 4.5 and 8 ϕ. The theoretical principle involved is Stokes's Law and the particle size measured is the Stokes diameter (p. 88). The method is accurate, though time–consuming, but if several pipettes are used at the same time, this increases speed and efficiency, since the experiment does not need continual restarting. The pipette measures the concentrated changes which occur within a settling suspension by withdrawing samples at fixed depths and time intervals.

The principle governing pipette analysis states that if two particles begin falling at the same time, the larger will fall faster than the smaller. Pipette samples taken at constant depth will therefore contain fewer and fewer coarse particles as settling time increases. The first sample theoretically determines the quantity of material in suspension, if this is not already known (Creager and Sternberg, 1963). This assumes total dispersion, which is seldom the case, and a further slight inaccuracy results from the fact that the withdrawal of samples does not take place quite instantaneously. Samples are taken to measure the concentration of chosen particle sizes, and are therefore spaced at $\frac{1}{4}$ or $\frac{1}{2}\phi$ intervals. Withdrawal heights and times must be corrected for temperatures and the other variables of the Stokes equation (p. 116). The theory can be illustrated by a simple example. At 20 °C a pipette sample taken at 10 cm depth and a time of 1 min 56 s after starting the experiment will contain particles finer than 5ϕ, but a similar sample taken at the same depth but after 7 min 36 s will contain material finer than 6ϕ. Table 10.3 shows the withdrawal heights and times

Table 10.3 PARTICLE SETTLING TIMES (AFTER GALEHOUSE, 1971)

Particle size (finer than φ units)	μm	Withdrawal depth (cm) below surface)	Withdrawal time		
			h	min	s
4	62.5	20	—	—	58
4.5	44.2	20	—	1	56
5	31.2	10	—	1	56
5.5	22.1	10	—	3	52
6	15.6	10	—	7	42
6.5	11·0	10	—	15	—
7	7.8	10	—	31	—
7.5	5.5	10	1	1	—
8	3.9	10	2	3	—
8.5	2.8	10	4	5	—
9	1.95	10	8	10	—
9.5	1.40	10	16	21	—
10	0.98	10	32	42	—

Temperature = 20 °C; specific gravity of particle = 2.65.

for $\frac{1}{2}\phi$ units; additional values may be calculated from the Stokes equation.

Since there are large time-gaps between the sample withdrawals in the finer grades, the apparatus may be left for long periods, so long as it remains undisturbed and at constant temperature. It is usual to take a pipette analysis down to 8ϕ, the silt/clay boundary, although analysis to 11ϕ is possible. However, since the 11ϕ reading would need to be taken some 65 h after the start of the experiment, this is not practical, and the use of a scanning electron microscope or high-speed disc centrifuge is recommended for samples with a high clay content. For archaeological purposes the tedious calculations may be much simplified. The cumulative percentage coarser than a given ϕ grade represented by each sample may be calculated from the following equation, if the correct experimental procedure has been carried out (Galehouse, 1971):

$$\text{cumulative \% of total sample} = 100 \times \frac{(A+B)-(C \times x)}{A+B} \quad (10.6)$$

where A = total weight of original sample (sieved material); B = weight of material processed by the pipette method; C = weight (after evaporation) of the individual pipette samples; and x = volume of the sedimentation cylinder divided by volume of the pipette. The cumulative percentage is then calculated for each pipette sample, and the results combined with the dry sieving results to give a complete size distribution curve, which may be

Site	WARSASH			Sample No.	WA/3/BRICK	Location	see map ref.	Date	13. 5. 71

Pre-treatment: *Removal of iron oxides, organic matter. Ultrasonic dispersion*
Previous analysis: *dry sieved*   Notes: —

Weight sieved: *543.284 g*   Weight sedimented: *20 g*   Dispersant: *Calgon*   Cylinder volume: *1000 ml*

Pipette volume: *20 ml*   Value of X: *50*   Specific gravity of particles: *2.65*   Temperature (°C): *20*

Clock time	Withdrawal time	Ø value	Depth	Weight of dish	Wt. of dish + sed.	Sed. wt. (C)	C x X
9 28 56	0 1 56	4.5	20	51.0973	58.9776	7.8803	394.015
(restart)							
9 30 -	0 1 56	5	10	51.5725	58.4743	6.9018	345.090
9 33 52	0 3 52	5.5	10	51.3623	54.5216	3.1584	157.920
9 37 42	0 7 42	6	10	51.7578	54.0280	2.2702	113.510
9 45 -	0 15 0	6.5	10	73.4947	73.8053	0.3106	15.530
10 1 -	0 31 0	7	10	72.8497	72.8497	0.1411	7.055
10 31 0	1 1 0	7.5	10	81.0267	81.1129	0.0912	4.560
11 33 0	2 3 0	8	10	67.3102	67.3461	0.0359	1.795

Fig. 10.1. Record sheet for pipette analysis. Example taken from a 'brickearth' from Warsash, near Southampton

drawn on arithmetic probability paper and processed by any of the methods described above (p. 100). A standard sheet for the recording of a pipette analysis is shown in *Figure 10.1*. The sample being processed was taken from a deposit of 'brickearth' which capped a low raised beach at Warsash, near Southampton, Hants. Since both the beach and the 'brickearth' contained Palaeolithic implements, it was important to know the environment of deposition of the latter, in case it represented the remains of a later marine transgression. The coarse fraction of the material had been dry sieved.

APPARATUS

The apparatus consists of an Andreasen pipette (Andreasen, Jensen and Lundberg, 1929) mounted on a stand with a movable rack (*Figure 10.2*). The pipette bulb, of either 20 or 25 ml capacity, is connected to the reservoir by a two-way tap, making it possible for the samples to be drawn up from a predetermined depth and then allowed to flow through an outlet tube into an evaporating dish, without disturbing the sedimentation cylinder. The suspension reservoir and outlet tube are then flushed through with distilled water from the clear fluid reservoir at the top of the instrument. The pipette is mounted in a clamp on the movable rack, which is attached to a stand calibrated in mm. The side arm may be attached to a simple suction pump, consisting of a vacuum tube joined to a tap, which can establish sufficient suction to withdraw a sample. This is superior to the use of a manual pipette since it enables precision of depth and timing to be obtained. The errors inherent in the pipette method, for example the 'shock' effect due to the impact of the pipette into the suspension, or the small sampling error resulting from the retention of sediment in the tube, are far less significant than those generated by any other sedimentation method. Since the temperature of the suspension is critical it is advisable either to keep the cylinder in a constant temperature water bath, or to ensure that the apparatus is in a draught-free position and that the laboratory temperature can be controlled. The former course is preferable, especially if the analysis is being carried out down to widely separated time intervals.

The method is as follows:

(1) The sample for analysis must be split and pre-treated by any of the methods described above. In practice it will often have been obtained as the pan fraction (finer than 4 ϕ) from dry sieve analysis; 15 or 20 g of the sample is then dispersed in distilled water, together with 15 ml of 10% 'Calgon', making a total volume of 1000 ml. If the initial weight of the sample is not known, or it is already in suspension, the 'initial aliquot' method of Creager and Sternberg (1963) must be used.

(2) Assemble the stand, suction pump and water-bath as shown in *Figure 10.2*. The temperature of the water-bath (and thus of the suspension) must remain constant. It is advisable to use a self-regulating

stirring thermometer in the water-bath[2] for this purpose. If the experiment is to last more than a couple of hours, both the cylinder and the water-bath should be covered to prevent evaporation. The writer has recorded evaporation losses of up to 5% of the total volume of sedimentation cylinder left uncovered overnight at normal laboratory temperature and without a water-bath. The

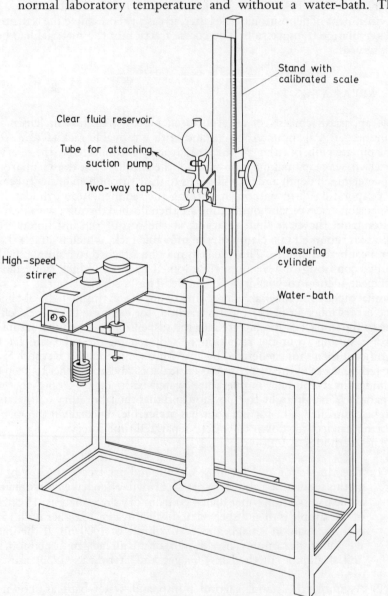

Fig. 10.2. Apparatus for a sedimentation analysis using the Andreasen pipette

whole apparatus must be positioned within reach of a tap for the suction pump.

(3) Decide on the required withdrawal heights and times, and enter these on the standard sheet (*Figure 10.1*). Note the pipette volume, water temperature, specific gravity and density of the fluid, and specific gravity of the sediment. Usually these will be constants.

(4) Ensure that the sample is adequately dispersed in the cylinder, by ultrasonics (p. 37) followed by use of an electric stirrer[2].

(5) Number and weigh a series of clean evaporating dishes, and switch the drying oven on to warm up. Connect the suction pump, flush the pipette through with distilled water and test the suction.

(6) Position the sedimentation cylinder in the water-bath under the pipette and lower the pipette until the tip just touches the surface of the suspension. Note the reading on the calibrated stand and use this to work out to what level the pipette must be sunk for the first reading, since this saves time. Leave the cylinder for a while to ensure that the temperature of water-bath and suspension is the same.

(7) Stir the suspension, start a stopwatch and turn the tap on to start the suction. Make sure that the tap is closed if the pipette tip is below water level. A sample is withdrawn by sinking the pipette to the required depth, using the graduated scale on the stand, opening the tap which fills the bulb by suction. As soon as the bulb is filled, close the tap. This time should coincide exactly with the calculated withdrawal time. The pipette is then slowly raised and the sample emptied into an evaporating dish via the two-way tap, care being taken not to allow any sediment to fall back into the cylinder. The reservoir and outlet tube are then flushed through into the evaporating dish with distilled water from the top reservoir. All taps are then closed and the suction pump is turned off.

(8) This last stage is repeated at the required time-intervals and depths. Since the first few samples are taken close together, it may be necessary to restart the experiment each time, by thoroughly stirring the suspension. This should be noted on the record sheet. It is usually impossible to complete the procedure in under $1\frac{1}{2}$–2 min, although this figure improves with practice.

With longer time-intervals it is good practice to try out the suction pump before the time at which a sample is due to be taken. If some fault has occurred and the critical time is passed, the whole experiment will have to be restarted. Occasional checks should also be made on the temperature of the water-bath, but a thermometer should not be stuck into the suspension, since this will disturb the settling of the particles. The suspension will rush up the tube very quickly once the tap to the suction pump has been opened, and it is advisable to keep one finger on the tap to close it instantly or the suspension reservoir will fill with unwanted sample. Samples are evaporated in a drying cabinet to constant weight, and placed in a desiccator before weighing. Weights are taken with an electronic balance, and accuracy to at least three decimal places is required. All results are noted on the standard sheet.

SEDIMENTATION USING A HYDROMETER

The hydrometer method is occasionally used for sedimentation analysis as an alternative to the pipette, but is considered to be less accurate, since errors are introduced due to displaced particles and faulty hydrometer readings. The method measures changes in the density of a settling suspension by direct readings taken from a hydrometer floating in the suspension. The volume of the hydrometer bulb, the meniscus and the dispersing agent correction factors and the cross-sectional area of the sedimentation cylinder must be calculated first (British Standard 3406(4): 1963; ASTM D422, 1963). The densities D_t are read off after a sedimentation time t, and the concentration of particles, C_t, is calculated from the formula

$$C_t = \frac{D_1}{D_1 - D_2} \times \left(D_t - D_2 \right) \qquad (10.7)$$

where D_1 = density of particles and D_2 = density of liquid. Curves have been developed which relate sinking times to density readings (Muhs, 1957). The method is not widely used at present but has recently been very successfully applied to archaeological sediments by Davidson (1973). He studied the evolution of the tell mound at Sitagroi (northeastern Greece) using a deep sounding. Thirty-seven samples were analysed for particle size distribution and total phosphate contents. A computer program for fitting Pearson curves was used to recognise particle size groupings. These groups were considered to reflect minor changes in the source of the local alluvium, which had been used for the construction of houses on the site, and clear correlations were evident between particle size groupings and occupation phases.

SEDIMENTATION USING SETTLING TUBES

Although the analysis of fine-grained materials is usually carried out by either the pipette or hydrometer technique, the use of settling tubes is becoming popular, since they are cheap to manufacture and very easy to use. Small quantities of material (approximately 2 g) are required, less than for either of the other methods. The most commonly used varieties of settling tube are the bottom withdrawal method of Kiff (1973) and the Stairmand sedimentation tube (Stairmand, 1950).

BOTTOM WITHDRAWAL SEDIMENTATION TUBE

This apparatus was first proposed in a publication of the University of Iowa (1943), and assessed by the St. Anthony Falls Hydraulic Laboratory

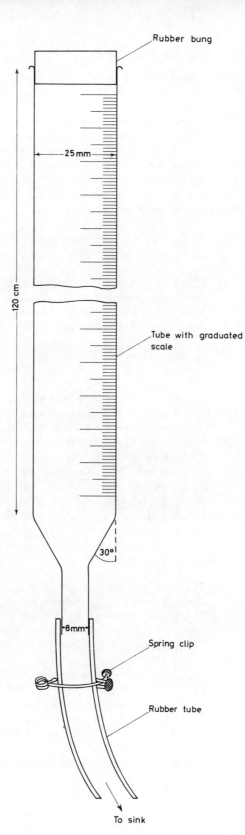

Fig. 10.3. Structure of a bottom withdrawal sedimentation tube

Rubber bung

25 mm

120 cm

Tube with graduated scale

30°

8 mm

Spring clip

Rubber tube

To sink

(1957). The method is favoured for sedimentation by the Hydraulics Research Station in Great Britain, and Kiff (1973) reviewed its applications.

The apparatus consists of a glass tube, about 120 cm long, with a constant internal diameter of 2.5 cm (*Figure 10.3*). One end is tapered to an outlet tube 8 mm in diameter, with a piece of soft rubber tubing attached. This is closed by means of a spring clip. A rubber bung is fitted to the top end of the tube, and the whole apparatus is supported in a clamp stand. The tube may be used for measuring particle size distributions of sediments finer than 4.5 ϕ by use of Stokes's Law.

CALIBRATION METHOD

(1) Close the spring clip on the outlet tube and position the tube upright in the clamp stand or rack. Add 20 cm³ of water through a funnel, bringing the water level to above the tapered portion of the tube. Mark this point on the glass. Add a further known volume of water (10 cm³ suffices) and calculate the volume of water per unit length of tube. Thus, if the difference in height was 5 cm and the second volume of water 10 cm³, the tube must contain 2 cm³ of water per 1 cm of length.

(2) Empty the tube by releasing the spring clip. Close the clip again and add water to correspond to a 5 cm length of tube. Mark this point permanently on the glass with a diamond marker.

(3) Make an accurate scale on a thin strip of paper and stick it firmly to the side of the glass tube, so that the tube is then graduated from 5 to 100 cm. Cover the scale with a coat of transparent nail varnish for protection. This calibration will be accurate so long as the tube is of regular bore and the position of the outlet tube and spring clip is not altered.

ANALYTICAL METHOD

(1) Take 1–4 g of the sample, after suitable pre-treatment. Add 100 ml distilled water. Close the spring clip on the tube and add the suspension. Make up to the 100 cm mark with distilled water to which 10 cm³ of 15% 'Calgon' has been added.

(2) Wash and weigh a series of centrifuge tubes or evaporating dishes.

(3) Replace the rubber bung in the top of the tube, remove it from the clamp and mix the suspension thoroughly by repeated inversions. The air bubble at the top acts as a mixing device. Withdrawal timing commences from the beginning of the last inversion.

(4) Replace the tube in the clamp and withdraw samples at predetermined intervals by removing the top bung and opening the bottom clip.

(5) The timing and frequency of sampling must be taken at selected

Temperature = 20°C

Column Number	1	2	3	4	5	6	7	8	9	10	11
	Reading No.	Height (cm)	Time	Wt. of evap. dish (g)	Wt. of dish + sample	Wt. of sediment	Cumulative wt.	Depth factor	Wt. in 100 cm of suspension	Corrected time (min)	% of total
	-	-	-	-	-	-	3.923	1.00	3.932	-	18.101
	1	86	100 (sec)	54.290	55.001	0.711	3.221	1.163	3.746	1.94	17.684
	2	72	3 (min)	48.806	49.502	0.695	2.526	1.389	3.508	4.17	16.946
	3	58	6	58.454	59.130	0.676	1.850	1.724	3.187	10.3	15.811
	4	44	12	53.992	54.613	0.621	1.228	2.273	2.782	27.3	11.898
	5	30	30	42.899	43.366	0.467	0.761	3.333	2.536	100	11.010
	6	15	90	39.963	40.400	0.437	0.324	6.667	2.160	600	5.608
	7	5	180	44.917	45.138	0.220	0.103	20	2.074	3 600	2.610
	8	0	180+	53.019	53.123	0.103	-	-	-	-	

Fig. 10.4. Record sheet for a bottom withdrawal sedimentation analysis

intervals (Kiff, 1973). A suitable sequence is shown in the first two columns of *Figure 10.4*. The level shown in column 2 must be reached at *exactly* the calculated withdrawal time, but this can easily be achieved with a little practice. After the final reading (180 min) the remaining sample is withdrawn down to the 5 cm mark into one container, and the rest run out into another. The timing and levels may be varied for particular temperatures. Samples are withdrawn into weighed vessels and evaporated to constant weight. The tube should be washed through with distilled water after use, and the temperature of the suspension should be checked periodically. If more than one tube is available, this speeds up the experiment, since it obviates the need for restarting.

(6) The weight of sediment in the sample is obtained after evaporation, and should be noted in Column 6 of *Figure 10.4*. The cumulative weight (Column 7) is obtained by adding the results of Column 6, starting at the bottom. The depth factor (Column 8) is applied to restore the cumulative weight and time to that required for a full 100 cm fall. It is obtained by dividing the results in Column 2 into 100. The corrected weight (Column 9) is found by multiplying Column 7 by Column 8. The corrected time (Column 10) may be found by multiplying the time (Column 3) by the depth factor (Column 8). The percentage in suspension (Column 11) is expressed as a percentage of the total weight.

The method has not yet been applied to archaeological samples, although its cheapness and simplicity are likely to prove useful. The results entered in the record sheet (*Figure 10.4*) are those obtained from the trial analysis of a floodloam. A simple graphical method of processing the results obtained is described by Kiff (1973). The particle diameter corresponding to the time of fall at various temperatures is obtained from the University of Iowa report (1943). The method is best used in combination with a dry sieve analysis.

STAIRMAND'S SETTLING TUBE

This method also allows of the analysis of smaller samples at lower concentrations than are required for pipette or hydrometer analysis. The apparatus consists of a sedimentation tube (*Figure 10.5*), a clear fluid reservoir and a thermal stabilising jacket (Stairmand, 1950). Approximately 0.1 cm^3 of the sediment is dispersed in 10 ml of fluid and transferred to the sedimentation tube. The mixture can be agitated by bubbling air through the tube (*Figure 10.5*). At recorded times the sedimented fraction is flushed out of the apparatus into a centrifuge tube, dried and weighed. The size distribution is derived from Stokes's Law in the usual way.

A more detailed discussion of the method may be found in Allen (1958). The apparatus is cheap and easy to operate, and has the advantage of minimising settling disturbance when sampling is done. Errors may be introduced, since the tubes are seldom accurately standard-bored. The speed of this method may also be increased if more than one tube is available.

The apparatus has been used successfully by several writers, notably Weir *et al.* (1971), who used it for determining the particle size distribution of a series of samples from a buried soil, developed in Weichselian loess at Pegwell Bay, Kent. The soil was radiocarbon dated to 6120 ± 250 BP. The composition of the sand and silt fraction suggested that only 10–20% of the

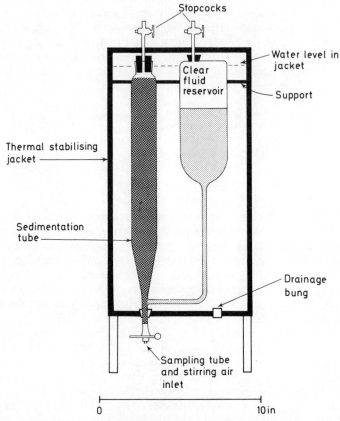

Fig. 10.5. Stairmand's settling tube for sedimentation (after Stairmand, 1950)

loess was derived from local material, the remainder having travelled some considerable distance. The soil profile had been buried by colluvium in late prehistoric times and most of the profile development appeared to have occurred during the post-glacial climatic optimum. The particle size analysis with this apparatus was supplemented by an examination of the soil in thin section, and by various chemical tests and a mineralogical analysis of the fine silts and clays by X-ray diffraction (p. 63).

Galehouse (1971) discusses the use of several varieties of settling tubes as alternatives to dry sieving. The advantages of his methods include a shorter analysis time, smaller bulk sample and increased mathematical sophistication. However, such tubes are seldom commercially available and are often expensive (Felix, 1969; Cook, 1969). Gibbs (1972) experimented with settling tubes of different heights and bores, commenting on the sample sizes required. He recommended a tube of 140 cm settling length, and internal diameter 13–16 cm, which would give accurate results with 1–2 g samples of sizes 0.3–2 mm diameter, and 0.6 g samples for grain sizes 0.02–0.5 mm. A much larger apparatus, the 'Bristol' fall column, was used by Channon (1971) for particle sizes 62 μm–8 mm in diameter. The sample size required was at least 50 g, in a fall tube 18 inches in diameter, and the results were expressed in terms of the fall velocity. The combination of results obtained with the finer sedimentation tubes and a dry sieve analysis has a certain incompatibility due to the different measures of particle 'size' being used, but no greater than that for any other combination of methods.

SEMI-AUTOMATED INSTRUMENTS FOR SEDIMENTATION ANALYSIS

SEDIMENTATION BALANCES

The first automatic sedimentation balance was described by Svendberg and Rinde (1934). It worked on the principle that as sediment accumulated on the pan of the balance, electrical points made contact and the current was fed into a motor which acted on the other arm to restore equilibrium. The time/current plot thus obtained was automatically recorded and later converted into a time/weight plot. Another variety of automatic balance working on a similar principle was developed by Pretorious and Mandersloot (1967).

The torsion balance described by Bostock (1952) is the most commonly used. Here the weight settling out of the suspension is read at chosen intervals of time directly from the deflection of the torsion wire. The manufacturers[20] have automated the device with a camera which photographs a scale, reading the deflection at fixed intervals. This automatic mode is very effective, and especially useful as the apparatus can be used to carry out analyses in the absence of the operator, or outside normal laboratory working hours. The balance requires a concentration of about 0.5 g of sediment per 250 ml of fluid, and will measure particle sizes from 5 to 75 μm. The automatic timing unit, which incorporates a camera using standard 35 mm black and white film, will switch off automatically 525 min after the beginning of the experiment. The method of calculating the results is quite simple and easily computerised (Bostock, 1952). The instrument is composed of a sedimentation tube, a thermal stabilising jacket and a receiving tank. The torsion balance mechanism is mounted on a heavy base and the apparatus should be positioned on a vibration-free bench. The principal advantage of the technique is the automatic mode.

THE EEL PHOTOEXTINCTION SEDIMENTOMETER[11]

The principle utilised by this instrument is a combination of gravitational settling with photoelectric measurements of the density variations in a suspension. The system will measure the particle size range 1–50 μm, again requiring initial sample sizes of less than 1 g. *Figure 10.6* illustrates its construction. It consists of a six-position cell holder mounted on a sliding

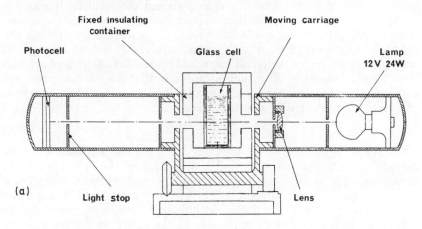

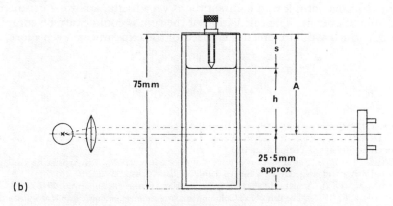

Fig. 10.6. (a) Structure and light path of the EEL photoextinction sedimentometer; (b) a glass test cell for the apparatus, standard dimensions. (Reproduced by courtesy of Evans Electroselenium Ltd)

carriage, which is positioned between two tubular chambers containing the optical system. The sediment is dispersed in glass test cells which are slotted into the holders, permitting of the processing of up to six samples at the same time. The narrow beam of light produced by the lamp passed directly through the glass wall of the cell, and through the suspension, at a fixed point, and its intensity is recorded by the photocell and outputted to a galvanometer attached to the apparatus. Control readings are taken from test cells filled with the clear suspension fluid (usually water), and experimental readings are then taken by noting the galvanometer readings from the different cells at predetermined size intervals. The variations in the attenuation of the beam of light due to the presence of particles in the suspension is therefore used to measure the particle size changes. The concentration of particles in the light beam at any one time will be the concentration of particles smaller than a chosen size (preferably $\frac{1}{4}$ to $\frac{1}{2}\phi$ units), and the particle size distribution is derived from the Stokes equation. Allen (1958) presents equations describing the mathematical basis of the method, and the instructions of the manufacturers[11] include a simplified way of calculating the results and a standard record sheet. The final product is a weight/frequency distribution using both Stokes's Law and the Lambert–Beer Law concerning the relationship between light attenuation and particle concentration in a suspension:

$$I = I_0 \exp\left(-TCL\right) \qquad (10.8)$$

where I, I_0 are the intensities of the emergent and incident radiation, T the turbidity, C the concentration and L the length of the light path in the suspension. The instrument is very useful for small samples of very fine material, especially silt, and the writer has used it successfully to process samples taken initially for pollen analysis from boreholes through lake sediments. It might also be applicable to the study of the particle size composition of potting clays and to archaeological problems where only a very limited sample size is available. The ability of the instrument to process more than one sample at the same time is very useful, and the instrument is simple to operate. The calculation of the results could easily be computerised, which would increase the speed of the experiments even more.

References

ALLEN, T. (1968). *Particle Size Analysis* (Halsted Press, London)
ASTM D422 (1963). 'Grain size analysis of soils' *1969 Book of ASTM Standards*, Vol. **11**, 205–216 (American Society for Testing Materials)
ANDREASEN, A. H. M., JENSEN, W. and V. LUNDBERG, J. J. V. (1929). 'Ein Apparat für die Dispersoidanalyse und einige Untersuchungen damit', *Kolloid-Z.*, **49**, 253–265
BOSTOCK, W. (1952). 'A new sedimentation balance', *Journal of Scientific Instruments*, **29**, 209
CHANNON, R. D. (1971). 'The Bristol Fall Column for coarse sediment grading', *Journal of Sedimentary Petrology*, **41** (3), 867–870
COOK, D. O. (1969). 'Calibration of the University of Southern California automatically recording settling tube', *Journal of Sedimentary Petrology*, **39**, 781–786
CREAGER, J. S. and STERNBERG, R. W. (1963). 'Comparative evaluation of three techniques of pipette analysis', *Journal of Sedimentary Petrology*, **33**, 462–466
DAVIDSON, D. A. (1973). 'Particle size and phosphate analysis—evidence for the evolution of a tell', *Archaeometry*, **15** (1), 143–152
FELIX, D. W. (1969). 'An inexpensive recording settling tube for analysis of sands', *Journal of Sedimentary Petrology*, **39**, 777–780
GALEHOUSE, J. S. (1971). 'Sedimentation analysis', in *Procedures in Sedimentary Petrology*, ed. Carver, R. (Wiley, New York)

GIBBS, R. J. (1972). 'The accuracy of particle size analyses utilizing settling tubes', *Journal of Sedimentary Petrology*, **42** (1), 141–145

IRANI, R. R. and CALLIS, C. F. (1965). *Particle Size Measurement, Interpretation, and Application* (Wiley, New York)

KIFF, P. R. (1973). 'Particle size analysis of sediments', *Laboratory Practice*, **6**, 259–267

KÖSTERS, E. (1960). *Mechanische Gesteins und Bodenanalyse* (München)

MUHS, H. (1957). *Die Prüfung des Baugrundes und der Böden* (Mitt. Deutsch. Forschunges Bodenmechanik, 11, Berlin)

MÜLLER, G. (1967). *Methods in Sedimentary Petrology* (Hafner, Stuttgart)

PRETORIOUS, S. T. and MANDERSLOOT, W. G. B. (1967). 'The Leschonski modification of the Sartorius sedimentation balance for particle size analysis', *Powder Technology*, **1** (1), 23–27

St. Anthony Falls Hydraulic Laboratory (1957). *A Study of Methods Used in Measurement of the Sediment Compounds in Streams, Report 16*: 'A study of the sediment size analysis made by the bottom withdrawal tube method'

STAIRMAND, C. J. (1950). 'A new sedimentation apparatus for particle size analysis in the sub-sieve range', in *Symposium on Particle Size Analysis*. Institute of Chemical Engineers and Society of the Chemical Industries of London

SVENDBERG, T. and RINDE, H. (1934). 'A sedimentation balance', *Journal of the Am. Chem. Society*, **45**, 173

University of Iowa (1943). *A Study of the Methods Used in Measurement and Analysis of Sediment Load in Streams, Report 7*: 'A study of new methods for size analysis of suspended sediment samples'

WEIR, A. H., CATT, J. A. and MADGETT, P. A. (1971). 'Postglacial soil formation in the loess of Pegwell Bay, Kent, England', *Geoderma*, **5**, 131–149

Chapter 11

PARTICLE SIZE ANALYSIS USING OPTICAL COUNTING METHODS

PARTICLE 'SIZE' AND SIZING METHODS

Particle size analysis using a light microscope involves the actual measurement of the dimensions of a number of particles to give a number/size distribution, namely the relative frequency of particles whose equivalent projected diameter (or other measurement of size) falls within certain size classes. Microscopy and other optical counting methods are generally considered to be the most accurate ways of obtaining a size distribution, because each particle is sized individually. However, care must be taken to ensure that the measured sample is truly random and fully representative of the original population.

The different meanings of the term particle 'size' have already been discussed (p. 88) and it is unfortunate that the various optical sizing methods tend to use different 'size' classifications. The commonest methods measure the equivalent projected diameter or nominal sectional diameter of the particle, by comparing it with a series of size classes (British Standard 3406, Part 4: 1963), or 'size' it by measuring one of the statistical diameters (such as Feret's or Martin's diameters), with a suitable calibrated eyepiece. Size analysis with a microscope is facilitated by the use of a microprojector or by the use of microphotographic techniques (Alling, 1941; Mandarino, 1956). Projection microscopes are made by the major optical companies and are particularly useful. They differ little in construction from standard light microscopes (p. 76) except that the image is projected on to a screen. Measurements may also be made by photographing the grain population and analysing the photomicrograph, a technique which has the advantage of providing a permanent record (p. 137).

The number of particles to be counted varies with the size range present, and it has been suggested that accuracy is best ensured by calculating the mean size of the particles as the count progresses (Irani and Callis, 1963), but this is a tedious process and usually unnecessary for archaeological purposes. Allen (1968) gives an equation for the calculation of the required number of particles that must be counted to give an accurate size distribution in any particular range.

134

Many papers have been written concerning the relationship between the measures of size determined microscopically and the volume or weight/size distributions obtainable by other methods. A transformation of number to weight distribution may be obtained by assuming that the particles are all spherical and have constant density. Rosenfeld, Jackobsen and Ferm (1955) determined the conversion factors for this transformation for several different sets of thin-section data obtained by particle size analysis of different rock types, and showed that the straight conversion of number to weight distribution by this method yielded coarser sizes than the correct values. Friedman (1958) obtained similar results.

The calculation of the projected area of the grain is probably the best method of sizing, although the use of the statistical linear diameters gives the most reproducible results. For archaeological purposes the use of either the Zeiss particle size analyser (p. 137) or the Humphries micrometer eyepiece (p. 138) (Humphries, 1966) is recommended over conventional hand counting methods. The latter apparatus has the advantage of retailing at approximately a quarter of the cost (c. £2000) of the former. If neither instrument is available, then the British Standard graticules provide a viable alternative, preferable to the tedious and boring method of making individual measurements of diameters with conventional micrometer scales. The use of automated particle measurement systems (p. 139) is an obvious solution, but these systems are barred from all but the richest laboratories by their prohibitive cost (£20 000 range).

SAMPLE PREPARATION FOR OPTICAL COUNTING

Measurements may be made either from grains visible in thin sections or from loose grain mounts obtained by any of the techniques described above (p. 52). The bulk sample will always require splitting, the microsplitter (p. 36) being particularly suitable for this purpose. The Canada Balsam mounting method (p. 52) is particularly suitable for small sand grains, although

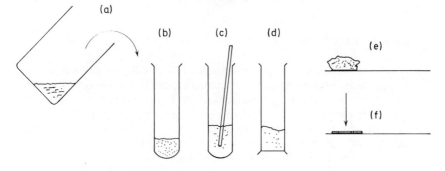

Fig. 11.1. Making a sand grain 'pudding': (a) pour prepared and treated grains into a small glass test tube (b); (c) add some industrial plastics[4] and stir well to disperse the grains, leave to set; (d) break the tube and extract the lump of mixture; (e) grind one face of the lump on a lap wheel and cement to a glass microscope slide; (f) after cement has set grind other face to standard thickness

consolidated fabrics are best mounted and thin sectioned (p. 82). Cornwall (1958) recommends the preparation of a mixture of 100 grains in a 'pudding' with Lakeside 70 or some other suitable material, which can be made in a glass test-tube and extracted by breaking the tube after the material has solidified. A thin section can then be cut and ground in the usual way (*Figure 11.1*). Good results are obtained by using industrial plastics, which dry extremely hard and are easier to work than Lakeside. They do not require heat, may be easily cut and have a drying time of a few hours. Mixtures made by this method should always be made in a breakable tube and never directly on to the microscope slide.

GRAIN SIZE MEASUREMENTS USING A GRATICULE

This method involves the examination of several hundred particles and comparing their projected areas with circles or discs of standard sizes, the projected area of the grains being recorded. The standards are usually engraved on a thin glass plate which can be inserted either into the microscope body or into the eyepiece. The most recent British Standard graticule (British Standard 3406, Part 4: 1963) has a series of reference circles in a $\sqrt{2}$ progression, designed as an extension of the sieve range. The method is therefore suitable for particles within the range c.4–10 ϕ (63–1.7 μm). Results are expressed as number/size distributions but may be converted to volume/size distributions with a corresponding loss of accuracy. The method is much faster than alternatives involving the accurate measurement of individual particles, but it tends to overestimate the size of flat grains. Several automated and semi-automated techniques are available for increasing the speed and accuracy of the work (p. 138), but these still require examination of at least 300–500 grains, and preferably more.

SEMI-AUTOMATED INSTRUMENTS USING A VARIABLE DIAPHRAGM

HORNSTEN'S APPARATUS

This semi-automated technique (Hornsten, 1959) will produce a number/size distribution. The instrument compares the area of a circle of light in the eyepiece with the grain image, the area of the light circle being controlled by the iris diaphragm on the microscope. The position of the lever controlling the iris is movable through a series of contacts and the size measured is recorded directly on to a bank of electromagnetic counters. The grain size is classified into one of ten size groups, covering the range from -1ϕ to $+7\phi$ (0.08–2 mm) on eight counters spaced at 1ϕ intervals, with an additional counter at each end to record particles over and under the size range. The large (1ϕ) class interval makes the resulting particle size analysis too coarse for accurate interpretation.

THE ZEISS TGZ3 SEMI-AUTOMATIC PARTICLE SIZE
ANALYSER[15]

This is another semi-automated instrument for determining particle size, which obtains the size distribution from photographic enlargements of the grain scatters, at the rate of 1000 particles per 15 min. The photograph, which may be an enlarged photomicrograph of a grain mount or a direct photograph of a scatter of coarse material, is placed on the sloping glass plate of the instrument, and an iris diaphragm of adjustable diameter is projected on to the plate and photograph. The different diameters of the diaphragm are correlated with a bank of 48 electromagnetic counters, each corresponding to a particular diameter range. The aperture must be adjusted to the projected area of the particle, and a foot switch depressed which activates the counter bank and a puncher which marks the measured particles. The instrument works in two ranges, 1.0–9.2 mm for narrow particle size distributions and 1.2–27.7 mm for wider distributions. Adjustments of the size distributions obtained must be made to allow for the magnification of the photograph.

The apparatus may be converted to an automatic mode and connected to data storage and processing units, which can be programmed to store data on paper tape or magnetic tape or as a digital printout. These data can then be fed straight into a computer for further analysis. This faculty is particularly useful, since it cuts out several of the data-processing stages and minimises data loss in transference. A further advantage of the instrument is the fact that the particles to be measured are selected by the operator, who can ignore agglomerations and take overlapping particles into account.

GRAIN MEASUREMENTS BY HAND COUNTING

COUNTING INDIVIDUAL PARTICLES

This method is particularly suitable for the size analysis of a particular mineral species, usually quartz, in a polymineralic thin section. The petrographic microscope used must have a mechanical stage (Chayes, 1949) to move the slide in a systematic way. Such a stage is manufactured by the optical companies to accompany their microscopes. The slide is traversed at a constant spacing and each grain of the required mineral that comes under the crossed hairs is measured with a calibrated micrometer eyepiece, until a pre-selected limit is reached. The use of an automatic counter bank, as described above, is strongly recommended. Friedman (1958, 1965) discusses this technique, which is unfortunately very time-consuming, since it involves the hand measurement of several hundred grains. Operators must remember to correct measurements for the magnifications used (p. 77). The 'random-cut' method of Münzer and Schneider-höhn (1953) is an improvement on the methods of Friedman.

THE HUMPHRIES EYEPIECE

The semi-automatic eyepiece described by Humphries (1966) combines speed, accuracy, ease of operation and a reasonable price[16]. Humphries worked on a principle, similar to the earlier thinking of Horsten (1959), that a very high degree of accuracy in optical sizing was not really required, since in any case the measurements were going to be grouped into classes, usually ϕ grades. The eyepiece that he developed has two hairlines appearing in the field of view, which are moved towards or away from each other by a milled head on the side of the apparatus. The lines are manipulated so that they just touch the sides of a grain, a push-button is depressed and the particle grade is recorded automatically into a bank of 16 electromagnetic counters (*Figure 11.2*) spaced for $\frac{1}{4}\phi$ units, a seventeenth

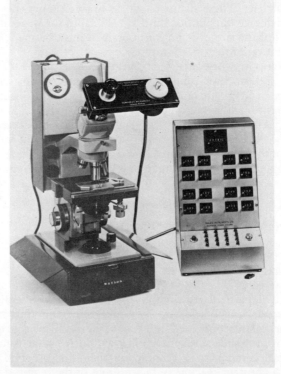

Fig. 11.2. The Humphries micrometer eyepiece mounted on a Watson microscope, with electromagnetic counter bank. (Reproduced by courtesy of Malies Scientific Instruments Ltd)

counter recording the total number of particles sized. The maximum error is less than 1% and the size range of particles that can be measured is governed by the objective and the magnification used. If a sample size range is very large, it may be necessary to count several times at different magnifications. Humphries estimated a count rate of 1000 grains/h, four or five times faster than point counting and far more accurate. The apparatus is highly recommended for archaeological purposes, and the data are obtained in a way that facilitates later mathematical treatment.

AUTOMATED IMAGE ANALYSIS

A number of fully automated particle analysers have been put on the market in recent years, including the PiMc (Millipore Ltd)[17], the Leitz Classimat (Leitz)[22] and the Quantimet 720M (Imanco). The operating principle of these is similar, and involves a particle image former (either a microscope or some form of macroscopic apparatus), monitoring the image with a scanning camera and feeding it into a computer which presents the required information on a data output system.

Figure 11.3 shows the PiMc system, operating in the microscopic mode. The instrument will give an automatic count of the total number of particles in a field of view, which appears on the television screen, and will measure parameters including the average particle area, total area and average projected length. By use of a light pen system individual particles can be selected on the screen and measured for Feret's diameter and the longest grain dimension. Measurement in this selective mode is still very rapid. A summary of the capabilities of the machine is given by Brown (1971). Count, measurements and size distributions may be obtained for a particle size range of several centimetres to 0.08 mm, by combining the macroscopic and microscopic modes in two successive operations. If the instrument is operating macroscopically, it can process a scatter of particles or a photographic enlargement, and in the microscopic mode will work on thin sections or particle mounts. Data are outputted either directly on to the size analysis module (*Figure 11.3*) or into a teletype. This system can usefully be combined with a small computer for data processing and for obtaining frequency distributions, and several attributes of the population —for example, grain size and shape—can be measured at the same time.

The trial processing of several archaeological samples was kindly undertaken by the manufacturers (Messrs. Millipore Ltd), which illustrated the potential of the machine. It is unfortunate that if the sample is very aggregated, processing on the automatic mode is unrealistic, and selective processing increases expensive machine time. A full size distribution of various archaeological sediments usually seemed to require a combination of the two size modes (macroscopic and microscopic), which is also time-consuming. The use of the light pen system for selecting individual particles for measurement was a particularly useful feature, as was the automatic data processing unit.

The cost of the machine runs into tens of thousands of pounds, and for this reason it is unlikely to become particularly widely used for archaeological purposes. However, it is possible to use the machine at a reasonable cost on a contract basis, and in future economic situations this type of arrangement might well be useful. On balance, however, it was not felt that the high cost of the machine was really outweighed by its advantages, and the

Fig. 11.3. The PiMC image analysing system, operating in the microscoping mode. The instrument includes the visual display screen, and modules to the left of the microscope for obtaining size distributions and measurements. (Reproduced by courtesy of Millipore Ltd)

use of semi-automated systems seems to be preferable for archaeological purposes, although the extreme accuracy offered by the instrument is a vitally important factor in many other branches of the physical and earth sciences.

References

ALLEN, T. (1968). *Particle Size Analysis* (Halsted Press, London)
ALLING, H. L. (1941). 'A diaphragm method for grain size analysis', *Journal of Sedimentary Petrology*, **11**, 28–31
British Standard 3406 (4): 1963. 'Optical Microscope Methods for the Determination of the Particle Size of Powders'
BROWN, J. F. C. (1971). 'Automatic microscopic analysis with the Particle Measurement computer', *The Microscope*, **19** (3), 285–299
CHAYES, F. (1949). 'A simple point counter for thin section analysis', *American Mineralogist*, **34**, 1–11
CORNWALL, I. W. (1958). *Soils for the Archaeologist* (Phoenix, London)
FRIEDMAN, G. M. (1958). 'Determination of sieve-size distributions from thin section data for sedimentary petrological studies', *Journal of Geology*, **66**, 394–416
FRIEDMAN, G. M. (1965). 'In defence of point counting analysis: a discussion', *Sedimentology*, **4**, 247–249
HÖRNSTEN, A. (1959). 'A method and a set of apparatus for mineralogical-granulometric analysis with a microscope', *Bull. Geol. Univ. Upsala*, **38**, 105–137
HUMPHRIES, D. W. (1966). 'Particle size measurement and a new semi-automatic recording eyepiece micrometer', *The Microscope*, **15**, 267–280
IRANI, R. R. and CALLIS, C. F. (1965). *Particle Size: Measurement, Interpretation and Application* (Wiley, New York)
MANDARINO, J. A. (1956). 'A new technique for micrometric analysis of thin sections', *American Mineralogist*, **41**, 786–789
MÜNZER, H. and SCHNEIDERHÖHN, P. (1953). 'Das Sehnenschnittverfahren', *Heidelberg. Beitr. Miner. Petrol.*, **3**, 456–471
ROSENFELD, M. A., JACKOBSEN, L. and FERM, J. C. (1955). 'A comparison of sieve and thin section techniques for particle size analysis', *Journal of Geology*, **61**, 114–132

Chapter 12

ALTERNATIVE METHODS FOR OBTAINING A SIZE DISTRIBUTION

ELECTRONIC PARTICLE SIZING: THE COULTER COUNTER

The Coulter Counter (*Figure 12.1*) is a rapid method for determining the number, size and weight of particles suspended in an electrolyte, by causing them to pass through a small-orifice tube with an electrode on either side. As the particles pass, the electric current path is slightly modulated, the resistance changes being proportional to the volume of the particle. The particles processed are counted and sized, and the method may be used to give accurate particle size distributions for fine materials. The instrument is currently used mainly for industrial purposes, and the

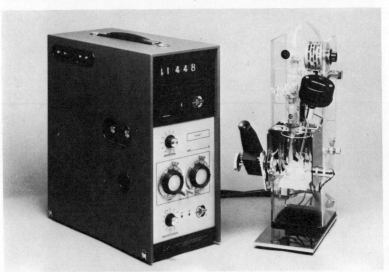

Fig. 12.1. The Model Zb Coulter Counter. (Reproduced by courtesy of Coulter Electronics Ltd)

manufacturers[21] publish an industrial bibliography which extends into several thousand papers.

Since sediments often have rather broad size distributions, compared with industrial powders, it is sometimes necessary to use several different orifice tubes in the instrument to complete one analysis and cover the complete size range. The most suitable Counters for this purpose are the Model D (industrial), which is relatively cheap and will analyse material in sub-sieve range from 1–75 μm, and the Model Zb fine particle analyser, which can cope with a broader size distribution from 0.6 to 300 μm. A weight and size distribution takes approximately 20 min on the Model D, and slightly less on the Zb. Particles are counted at a rate of 5000/s and the results are reproducible to $\pm 1\%$. The instruments are available on a contract basis from various laboratories to deal with archaeological samples.

SPECIMEN ANALYSIS USING A COULTER COUNTER

Figure 12.2 shows a table of the results obtained from the analysis of two samples, which was kindly undertaken by the manufacturers of the Coulter Counter. The samples were taken from the extensive deposits of 'brickearth' which underlie the Saxon town of Hamwih, at Southampton, Hants. The excavator of the site required a description of the texture and composition of this material, since nearly all the archaeological remains of the town (postholes, trenches, pits, gullies, etc.) are dug into it. The brickearth rests conformably on gravel deposits at a height of approximately 0–3 m O.D., in the Northam/St. Mary's area of Southampton, and is

Sample 'brickearth'. Hamwih Sample A			Sample 'brickearth' Hamwih Sample B		
Orifice tubes 280, 100, 30μm Dispersion Nomidet P42 Ultrasonics			Orifice tubes 280, 100, 30μm Dispersion Nomidet P42 Ultrasonics		
Equivalent particle diameter (m)	No. of particles above size D	Cumulative % wt. above D	Equivalent particle diameter (m)	No. of particles above size D	Cumulative % wt. above D
Fine sand 102	16	8·65	102	18	6.99
80.6	28	11·9	80.6	49	12.8
64.0	72	17·8	64.0	115	19.4
50.8	188	25·4	50.8	282	27.2
40.3	406	33·0	40.3	583	34.6
32.0	928	41·6	32.0	1301	43.5
25.4	1927	50·3	25.4	2616	51.3
20.2	3729	57·8	20.2	4859	58.3
Silt 16.0	6669	63·8	16.0	8831	64.1
12.7	10992	68·6	12.7	15513	69.1
10.1	18619	72·4	10.1	27805	73.4
8.00	32667	75·9	8.00	48730	77.1
6.35	57563	78·9	6.35	85269	80.4
5.04	103538	81·9	5.04	152239	83.3
4.00	183317	84·3	4.00	268197	85.8
3.17	339898	86·5	3.17	510451	88.2
2.52	647136	88.4	2.52	961527	90.3
2.00	1265544	90.3	2.00	1749063	92.2
Clay 1.59	2582798	92.4	1.59	3361947	94.2
1.26	5256619	94.6	1.16	6293792	95.9
1.00	10414051	96.8	1.00	11713496	97.5
0.79	19357228	98.6	0.79	21032775	98.8
0.63	33108566	100	0.63	35721540	100

Fig. 12.2. Specimen record sheet for a Coulter Counter analysis. Example taken from the analysis of two weathered loess samples from Hamwih, Southampton

without any internal stratigraphy or structure. The exact distribution of the deposit is not known, since the 6 in Geological maps (Drift series) are very inaccurate, and the area is very heavily built up. The deposit was considered either as part of the extensive series of sediments in S. England which are all described as 'brickearth', although they include many different types of deposit, such as flood loams, weathered podsols and dune sands, or else to be the result of sedimentation from a tidal lagoon, which Crawford (1949) suggested might have been present at the time of the occupation of Hamwih. The problem was therefore to describe the characteristics of the sediment and to define its depositional environment, since the presence or absence of the lagoon is obviously a critical factor in the interpretation of the excavated town plan.

It was decided to undertake a detailed particle size analysis of two major samples, using the Coulter Counter, accompanied by supplementary analyses of a series of smaller samples and a description of the general features of the sediments in the field and the laboratory. The two samples (labelled A and B) were selected from exposures of the brickearth in ex-cavated areas, a random sampling plan based on a grid system being used. The sampling points were separated by nearly 500 m. Subsidiary samples were taken along the same grid. The brickearth was less than 2 m thick at the sampling points, and samples were taken from mid-points in the stratigraphy. No soil development was present, although in other areas the presence of a thin, decalcified *braunerde* has been reported.

The main samples were processed initially by ultrasonic dispersion, and sized in the Counter Zb, using three different orifice tubes of sizes 280 μm, 100 μm and 30 μm. The particles counted exceeded 3×10^6 per sample. The results of the analysis are shown in *Figure 12.2* as weight percentages, and are plotted as cumulative percentage frequency distributions on arithmetic probability paper in *Figure 12.3*. The Inclusive Graphic statistics of Folk and Ward (1957) were then calculated from percentile values read from the curve, and are summarised below in *Table 12.1*.

Table 12.1 PARAMETER VALUES FOR THE HAMWIH 'BRICKEARTHS'

Measurement	Sample A	Sample B
Mean (M_Z)	0.40	0.45
Standard deviation (σ_1)	2.139	1.932
Skewness (Sk)	0.377	0.136
Kurtosis (K_G)	6.557	7.259

The mean sizes of both samples fall in the fine sand/silt range, both are positively skewed and have high values of kurtosis. It has already been noted that beach sands and material processed in a highly dynamic environment tend to be negatively skewed, and that the higher the value of the kurtosis the lower the energy of the depositional environment. Such high kurtosis values could apply to either estuarine or aeolian sediments, but in this case the unimodal nature of the size distribution (*Figure 12.2*) and the poor sorting support the latter suggestion. Over 50% of each sample is composed of silt, the remainder being fine sand and clay. *Figure 12.3* shows that both samples are remarkably similar in composition, Sample B being slightly finer. This high silt content and the general size distributions were taken by Pitcher, Spearman and Pugh (1954) and Dues, Holmes and Robbie (1954) as characteristic of aeolian-deposited loess. The slight difference in the percentage of clay between the samples might be attributable to weathering *in situ*, since Cornwall (1958) noted that the percentage of clay

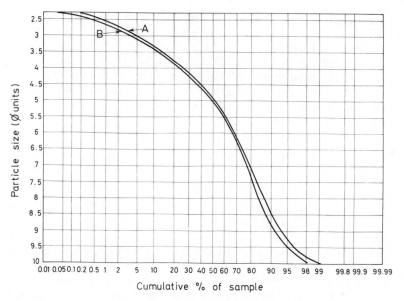

Fig. 12.3. Particle size distribution curves (arithmetic probability paper) of the two samples tabulated in Fig. 12.2

in loess tended to increase at the expense of the sand fraction if the material was weathered. The smaller samples taken from other points in the area confirm these general trends, and are all remarkably similar in composition. It is suggested that the material probably forms part of the Younger Loess, formed during some phase of the Weichselian (Devensian) glaciation at the end of the Pleistocene (Swanson, 1968). The size distribution curves are quite different from those obtained from fluviatile sediments such as flood loams, and the individual grains show none of the features associated with water action and many of those suggested by Krinsley and Doornkamp (1973) as indicative of wind action. Other deposits of weathered loess are known from the Southampton area—for example, those described by Swanson (1968) and Everard (1952) at Holbury and Nursling, both of which are also mapped as 'brickearth'. However, other 'brickearths' in the immediate area include estuarine silts and weathered podsols, which are texturally quite distinct from the loess. In view of the distance between the sampling points and the general uniformity of the material it seems reasonable to conclude that the 'brickearths' underlying Hamwih are weathered deposits of loess, not estuarine silts.

The archaeological implications of this conclusion are considerable, since reliance had been placed on the theory of Crawford (1949) that the Saxon town was bounded in the south-west by a tidal creek leading to a lagoon. All the samples analysed were taken from *inside* the area of the supposed lagoon, and both Crawford (1949) and Addyman and Hill (1968) seem to have identified the 'brickearth' with estuarine silts. Excavations at two sites (Sites 25 and 26, in Addyman and Hill, 1968) produced material described as 'presumably lagoonal silts' and 'fine apparently waterlain silts above gravel'. It is suggested that the complete lack of any sedimentological evidence for estuarine deposits and the uniformity of the weathered loess both inside and outside the area of the supposed lagoon point to a misinterpretation of the environment of deposition of the 'brickearth'. To dispense with the lagoonal theory necessitates a review of the postulated boundaries of the Saxon town, and the whole study illustrates the case made earlier for integration between excavation and analysis.

FISHER'S AIR PERMEABILITY METHOD

The 'air permeability' method of Fisher (1968) provides a convenient technique for comparing the textures of different batches of the same material, although it does not permit of detailed characterisation of the sediment, since a full size distribution is not obtained. Measurements are made by packing a unit value of solid material between porous plugs in a precision-bored tube, and then blowing air through the bed and measuring the pressure drop. The pre-calibrated instrument used gives a direct reading of mean particle size, but no further information about the size distribution.

The theoretical basis of the method rests on the fact that the pressure drop across a packed bed of material depends on the mean size of the voids between the particles, and not on the size of the particles themselves. Two sediments with the same size distribution but with different particle shapes will therefore give different results, since the particles would be 'packed' differently and would appear to have different sizes. The method seems to have little archaeological application at present.

ELUTRIATION

Elutriation is the process of grading particles by an upward current of fluid, usually either water or air. The process is the reverse of gravity sedimentation, and Stokes's Law still applies. The grading is carried out in a series of vessels of increasing diameter, so that the fluid velocity increases at each stage, leaving the coarsest particles in the smallest vessel and the finer ones in progressively larger vessels. The classic apparatus for air elutriation is described by Roller (1931) and an alternative method (Mills, 1970) is particularly suitable for the analysis of clays. Elutriation requires rather bulky apparatus and the technique has few advantages over sedimentation methods such as the Andreasen pipette method.

CENTRIFUGAL METHODS

The use of a centrifuge is common for the analysis of very fine material, usually clays with particle sizes of less than 5 μm. Such fine material has a long settling time in gravitational sedimentation, and makes sieving impossible and optical microscopy very time-consuming. Electron microscopy remains the only other workable alternative. In centrifugal analysis sedimentation from a suspension of particles in a liquid is accelerated and the size calculated from the settling rate. In the majority of centrifuge methods the solids are obtained from the suspensions by drying and weighing, and the calculations for obtaining the particle size distribution are carried out in a manner similar to that already described for the Andreasen pipette (p. 118).

Early workers used standard laboratory centrifuges, but the larger disc centrifuge (Kaye, 1966), which is commercially available, is far more accurate. The instrument measures concentration changes within a suspension of the sediment by use of a light beam, and a series of analyses can be carried out without it being necessary to switch off the instrument. The centrifuge is usually connected to a data-collection device which will provide an automatic printout of the particle size distribution. The process works on the two-layer principle described by Allen (1960), on an incremental basis, and determines the fraction sedimented against time.

The exact composition of the clay fraction is seldom required for archaeological purposes, and the disc centrifuge is too expensive to form a standard item of laboratory equipment. The range limits of the Kaye centrifuge (0.1–30 μm) leaves an annoying gap between the lower sieve limit and upper centrifuge limit. The MSA particle size analyser (Allen, 1960) solves this problem with an extended working range of 0.1–80 μm, but is not so easily available. However, if a large number of clay-rich samples are to be analysed, the contract use of either a centrifuge or an electron microscope is recommended. The latter has the disadvantage of being slower and not having an automatic data processing system. The analysis of clay-rich material should never be attempted with an Andreasen pipette, since each operation will take at least several days and results become extremely inaccurate.

References

ADDYMAN, P. V. and HILL, D. H. (1968). 'Saxon Southampton. A review of the evidence. Part 1. History, location, date and character of the town', *Proceedings of the Hampshire Field Club*, **25**, 61–93
ALLEN, T. (1968). *Particle Size Analysis* (Halsted Press, London)
CORNWALL, I. W. (1958). *Soils for the Archaeologist* (Phoenix, London)

CRAWFORD, O. G. S. (1949). 'Trinity Chapel and Fair', *Proceedings of the Hampshire Field Club*, **17**, 45–55

DUES, H. G., HOLMES, S. C. and ROBBIE, J. A. (1954). 'Geology of the country around Chatham', *Mem. Geological Survey*

EVERARD, C. E. (1952). 'A contribution to the geomorphology of south Hampshire and the Isle of Wight', unpublished M. Phil. Thesis, University of London

FISHER, P. (1968). 'Research on particle size', *Pharmaceutical Journal*, **201**, 177–181

FOLK, R. L. and WARD, W. C. (1957). 'Brazos river bar. A study in the significance of grain size parameters', *Journal of Sedimentary Petrology*, **27**, 3–26

KAYE, B. H. (1966). 'Determining the characteristics of fine powders', *Chemical Engineering*, **73**, 239–245

KRINSLEY, D. H. and DOORNKAMP, J. C. (1973). *Atlas of Quartz Grain Surface Textures* (Cambridge University Press)

MILLS, W. H. JR. (1970). 'Suggested method for grain size analysis of soils by eleutriation' in *Special Procedures for Testing Soils and Rocks for Engineering Purposes* (5th ed.), ASTM Technical publication 479

PITCHER, W. S., SPEARMAN, D. J. and PUGH, D. C. (1954). 'The loess of Pegwell Bay, Kent', *Geological Magazine*, **91**, 308–314

ROLLER, P. S. (1931). 'Separation and size distribution of microscopic particles: an analyser for finer particles', *US Bureau of Mines, Technical Publication*, 490

SWANSON, E. H. (1968). 'Pleistocene geochronology in the New Forest, Hampshire', *Bulletin of the Institute of Archaeology, University of London*, **8–9**, 55–101

APPENDIX: MANUFACTURERS

(1) Munsell Colour Company of America,
2441 North Calvert Street,
Baltimore, Maryland, USA
Tintometer Sales Ltd.
(English Agent for Munsell),
Waterloo Road,
Salisbury, Wiltshire

(2) Engineering Laboratory Equipment Ltd,
Durrants Hill Trading Estate,
Apsley, Hemel Hempstead,
Herts.

(3) May and Baker Laboratory Chemicals Ltd,
Dagenham RM10 7XS, Essex

(4) Quentsplass Ltd,
Boston Spa LS23 7BZ, Yorks.

(5) Drix Plastics Ltd,
Richmond Gardens,
Southampton, Hants.

(6) Cutrock Engineering Co. Ltd,
35, Ballards Lane, London, N3

(7) James Swift and Son Ltd,
Joule Road,
Houndmill Industrial Estate,
Basingstoke, Hants.

(8) Ultrasonics Ltd,
Otley Road,
Shipley BD18 2BN, Yorks.

(9) Cambridge Scientific Instruments Ltd,
Chesterton Road,
Cambridge CB4 3AW

(10) Pye-Unicam Ltd,
York Street,
Cambridge CB1 2PX

(11) Evans Electroselenium Ltd,
Halstead CO9 2DX, Essex

(12) (The 'Karbonat-Bombe'),
c/o Professor G. Müller,
Laboratorium für Sediment-
forschung,
Mineralogisch-Petrographisches
Institut der Universität,
69 Heidelberg, Berliner Strasse,
West Germany

(13) McCrone Research Associates Ltd,
2 McCrone Mews,
Belsize Lane, London NW3 5BG

(14) Wild Heerbrugg Ltd,
CH-9435 Heerbrugg,
Switzerland

(15) Carl Zeiss (Oberkochen) Ltd,
Degenhardt House,
31–36 Foley Street,
London W1P 8AP

(16) Malies Scientific Instruments Ltd,
St Ann's Place, Southwick,
Brighton BN4 4EA, Sussex

(17) Millipore (UK) Ltd,
Millipore House,
Abbey Road,
London NW10 7SP

(18) The Pascall Engineering Co. Ltd,

Gatwick Road,
Crawley RH10 2RS,
Sussex

(19) Beckman–RIIC Ltd,
Eastfield Industrial Estate,
Glenrothes KY7 4NG,
Scotland

(20) Gallenkamp & Co. Ltd,
P.O. Box 290,

Technico House,
London EC2P 2ER

(21) Coulter Electronics Ltd,
High Street South,
Dunstable LU6 3HT, Beds.

(22) E. Leitz Ltd,
48 Park Street,
Luton LU1 3HP, Beds.

AUTHOR INDEX

SUBJECT INDEX

155